the Blessed Virgin Mary

The month of May
Consecrated to the glory of the Mother of God, the Queen of Heaven, etc

ISBN/EAN: 9783742864765

Manufactured in Europe, USA, Canada, Australia, Japa

Cover: Foto ©Lupo / pixelio.de

Manufactured and distributed by brebook publishing software (www.brebook.com)

the Blessed Virgin Mary

The month of May

HAIL, HOLY QUEEN! OUR LIFE! OUR SWEETNESS! OUR HOPE!

THE MONTH OF MAY:

CONSECRATED TO THE

Glory of the Mother of God, the Queen of Heaven.

CONTAINING

PRACTICAL REFLECTIONS FOR EVERY DAY OF THE MONTH AND OF HER FESTIVALS DURING THE YEAR.

Dedicated to the Children of Mary.

LONDON:
BURNS AND OATES, PORTMAN STREET, W.

PREFACE.

MAN'S life on earth is a warfare, commenced in the terrestrial paradise, to terminate only on the threshold of the heavenly Jerusalem. God watches over the Church, His spouse, and over man, His beloved child; He proportions assistance to the violence of attacks, so that victory is always on the side of religion, that is, of truth and virtue. Thus, every century has a remedy proper for its evil, every heresy is opposed by a defender of truth, every scandal by a victim of expiation.

But above all remedies, there is one applicable to all evils; above all defenders of truth and virtue, there is, possessing equally strength and goodness, always ready to combat, and ever victorious—MARY! Mary, who crushed the serpent's head; Mary, who triumphed over all heresies and over all scandals. Therefore, the and of flowers be one of tepidity or sin. From the first day to the last, let each ask herself—If Mary were in my place to-day, how would she act? What would be the modesty of her looks, the affability of her manner, the meekness of her words, the promptitude of her obedience, the charity of her conversation, the recollection of her prayer, the purity of her intention; in one word, the sanctity of her conduct.

The Month of Mary is but a particular manifestation of the devotion professed towards the most holy Virgin, in every age, by the Church of God. Ever ready to encourage pious practices, she was not slow to enrich this with Indulgences.

By a rescript of 21st March, 1815, Pope Pius VII., of holy memory, granted to those who make the Month of Mary three hundred days' Indulgence for each day, and a Plenary Indulgence for one on which they shall communicate. Now, more than ever, the state of the Church, of society, and families, requires the assistance of Mary; it is time, more than time, to unite with her most devoted children. No more than man, can society or families go to God without Mary; no family or society devoted to Mary shall perish. This is the watchword of centuries, the voice of experience, the testimony of faith. What need we more? "All good things came to me together with her, and innumerable riches through her hands."*

Let us offer ourselves unreservedly to her for life, and more especially for death, saying with Henry Boudon—O amiable and most holy Mother of God, never sufficiently loved! O Virgin of Virgins, immaculate from the first moment of your conception, how sweet to die, in any way, at your feet! There let me live; there let me die! This is the grace, O my sweet and faithful Mother, which I ask of you in all humility.

* Wisdom vii. 11.

CONTENTS.

	PAGE
Preface	vii
Eve of the Month of Mary.—Invitation to celebrate with fervour the Month of Mary	1
First Day.—Origin and Practice of the Month of Mary	6
Second Day.—How we are to honour Mary	14
Third Day.—Antiquity of Devotion to the Holy Virgin	18
Fourth Day.—Devotion to Mary is the most sure Pledge of Perseverance	23
Fifth Day.—Mary is our Mother	28
Sixth Day.—The great Love borne to us by Mary our Mother	32
Seventh Day.—The Confidence we ought to have in Mary	38
Eighth Day.—Mary is Queen of Mercy	46
Ninth Day.—Mary is the Consolation of the Afflicted	52
Tenth Day.—Mary is the Refuge of Sinners	62

Contents.

	PAGE
Eleventh Day.—Mary aids those who invoke her in Temptation	72
Twelfth Day.—Mary is the Terror of Demons	78
Thirteenth Day.—Mary is our Mediation	83
Fourteenth Day.—Mary is our Advocate	87
Fifteenth Day.—Mary's Power	92
Sixteenth Day.—All Good Things come to us through Mary	98
Seventeenth Day.—Mary succours her Servants in their last moments	106
Eighteenth Day.—Mary succours her Servants in Purgatory	112
Nineteenth Day.—Mary is the Gate of Heaven	118
Twentieth Day.—The Holy Name of Mary	123
Twenty-first Day.—On the Immaculate Heart of Mary	127
Twenty-second Day.—Immaculate Conception of Mary — sublime sanctity to which she was elected	133
Twenty-third Day.—Mary teaches her Servants how to Pray	139
Twenty-fourth Day.—Mary conducts us to Jesus	146
Twenty-fifth Day.—Tokens whereby we may discover if we love Mary	152
Twenty-sixth Day.—The true Servant of Mary should condole with her Sorrows	158
Twenty-seventh Day.—The Client of Mary should be devoted to the Salvation of Souls	162

Contents.

	PAGE
Twenty-eighth Day.—The true Child of Mary should imitate her Virtues	171
Twenty-ninth Day.—Fidelity to our Devotional Exercises to Mary	176
Thirtieth Day.—Of the Zeal that Mary expects from her Children in making her known and loved	181
Thirty-first Day.—Consecration to Mary	185

Visits to the Blessed Sacrament during the Month of May.

First Visit	192
Second Visit	193
Third Visit	194
Fourth Visit	195
Fifth Visit	197
Sixth Visit	198
Seventh Visit	199
Eighth Visit	200
Ninth Visit	201
Tenth Visit	202
Eleventh Visit	203
Twelfth Visit	204
Thirteenth Visit	206
Fourteenth Visit	207
Fifteenth Visit	208
Sixteenth Visit	209
Seventeenth Visit	210
Eighteenth Visit	211

Contents.

	PAGE
Nineteenth Visit	212
Twentieth Visit	212
Twenty-first Visit	213
Twenty-second Visit	214
Twenty-third Visit	216
Twenty-fourth Visit	217
Twenty-fifth Visit	218
Twenty-sixth Visit	218
Twenty-seventh Visit	220
Twenty-eighth Visit	221
Twenty-ninth Visit	221
Thirtieth Visit	223
Thirty-first Visit	224
Anima Christi	225
Short Act of Consecration to the Sacred Heart of Jesus	225
Memorare	226
O Domina Mea	226
Ave Maris Stella	227
Prayer to our Lady of Sorrows	228
A Prayer to be said every day during May	228
Exercise to unite oneself to the Passion during the Holy Sacrifice of the Mass	230

THE MONTH OF MAY.

EVE OF THE MONTH OF MARY.*

INVITATION TO CELEBRATE WITH FERVOUR THE MONTH OF MARY.

"Behold now is the acceptable time, behold now is the day of salvation" (2 Cor. vi. 2).

CHRISTIANS, be you just or sinners, this is the favourable time for you to recur to the Divine Mercy; these are days offered you by Mary in her ardent desire to promote your salvation and perfection. "Behold now is the acceptable time, now is the day of salvation." Mary invites you to avail yourselves thereof in these touching words placed on her lips by Holy Church. "Come over to me all you that desire me, and be filled with my

---

* His Holiness Pius VII., by a rescript dated 21st March, 1815, grants to all the Faithful who will perform some devotion, whether public or private, or some other work of piety in honour of the Blessed Virgin, daily during the month of May, three hundred days indulgence each time, and a plenary indulgence on any day at their own option, on the usual conditions. These indulgences are applicable to the souls in Purgatory.

fruits."* "He that shall find me, shall find life, and shall have salvation from the Lord."† Not the life of a day in which so many ills are crowded, but of that life of bliss of which no created intellect, how vast soever its capacities, can form any conception. "To-day if you should hear her voice, harden not your heart."‡ Though Mary invariably comes to the aid of her suppliants at whatever time or season they may invoke her, she is pleased, nevertheless, to render these days an especial period of grace, during which she showers down the most signal favours on mankind. Now is the time to ask, to obtain all. We do not form to ourselves a sufficiently ample idea of Mary's omnipotence, of her desire to grant our petitions. We ask little, and even in asking this little, we are neither confiding, importunate, nor persevering.

Let us then dilate our heart, Mary will fill it—"Open thy mouth, and I will fill it."§ Let us ask great graces during this month, let us ask them with confidence, and persist in urging our request during all these days of mercy; we shall see if the arm of Mary be shortened, if her power, her love for us, are not to-day such as our fathers have described them to be.

If the Lord has deigned to promise, that where two or three are gathered together in His name, He will be in the midst of them, what may we not expect from the Mother of Mercy, now that she sees the entire Catholic world prostrate at her feet, imploring her aid, offering a sweet violence to her maternal Heart? Wherever the Name of Jesus has penetrated, the sweet name of Mary resounds this

---

* Eccles. xxiv. 26.   ‡ Psalm xciv. 8.
† Prov. viii. 35.   § Psalm lxxx. 11.

lovely month. All over Europe, amid the numerous and fervent missions of Asia and of the coasts of Africa, throughout the length and breadth of America, it is invoked. From the midst of lands a prey to heresy, the voices of many fervent Catholics blend with those of their brethren in other climes, so that we may say, from the east to the west an uninterrupted concert of prayer ascends to the Mother of Mercy the whole month long, whilst from the maternal Heart innumerable graces descend upon her children. Who would remain silent and refuse to join in this universal supplication? Who would remain with empty hands and hearts in this abundance of spiritual goods? Let us, then, present our homage at the feet of our Queen, of our Mother; let us rival in zeal the many souls devoted to Mary, and let us endeavour not to be surpassed in love, in fidelity, in generous sacrifices.

Poor abandoned souls—learned, ignorant, great, lowly, weak, ill, sinners—come! All ye children of Adam, whatever your rank and condition, come all, from pole to pole! Come, for the salvation of souls, have recourse to the liberal and omnipotent providence of Mary; implore the intercession of her who was chosen to impart temporal life to the Divine Word. Come, and delay not, lest the gates of Heaven be closed against you, for your sins place bolts on the divine mercy. Come, press on in haste, since it is the intercession of God's Mother that alone prevents those bolts from closing the portals of Heaven; for Mary alone is sufficiently powerful to plead for and to obtain your salvation; she is Heaven's open gate, which even your iniquities cannot close—*Quæ pervia cæli porta manes*. O nations redeemed by the Blood of a God, hail your liberatrix, and applaud the homages rendered to her. *Gentes redemptæ plaudite!* If you possess true faith, to her you owe it; have you forfeited it, she invites you to embrace it anew, she extends her arms to you, and longs to fold you to her Heart; are you still seated in darkness, in the shadow of death, take courage, it is she who urges on the steps of those apostolic men who are destined to introduce you one day into the fold of her Divine Son.

Practice.—Enter on this month with renewed fervour, and contribute, as much as lies in your power, to promote this solid Devotion to Mary, especially in those places where it has not hitherto been observed. Assist, if possible, at the exercises publicly carried on in the church; but if this be inconvenient, erect an altar to Mary at home, and go there daily, to pay her your tribute of homage.

Example.

Wherever the Devotion of the Month of Mary has been established, the results have been most striking. Hear what an ecclesiastic wrote a few years ago to the Curé of Notre Dame des Victoires —"Placed by Providence at the head of a parish numbering nearly four thousand souls, I struggled with but little success against the torrent of iniquity which had invaded, and was gradually sapping, the foundations of religion among my flock. For eighteen years had I presided over them, and all my efforts had been nearly fruitless. What to do I knew not; when suddenly the thought occurred to me that my parish was under Mary's protection. It occurred to me, I say, for to my confusion be it confessed, my devotion to this tender Mother had been, up to this time, very superficial, and, like many young people of ardent temperament, I relied too much on my own weak efforts.

"The more promptly to repair the harm my presumption had inflicted on my flock, I hastened to instruct them concerning the mercies of this good Mother, and I established the 'Month of Mary.' From that moment the face of things became quite changed. During this month of benediction, every evening saw my church thronged by from fifteen to eighteen hundred persons of every age and sex, some of whom came from the most distant parts of the parish—sometimes two leagues—to join in canticles to Mary, and hear a sermon on her benefits and virtues. The custom of swearing was abolished, licentious discourses and songs were no longer to be heard. Under Mary's patronage I gave my young men a little retreat. Nearly all have approached the Holy Table, and have persevered for more than a year in their good resolutions. I also gave a retreat to the young girls, and every Sunday after Vespers I have the consolation of seeing more than three hundred assemble in a private chapel to hear a special instruction from me. Each rivals the other in zeal to acquire those virtues which form the ornament of their age and the happiness of life."

Aspiration.—

> Sing, ransomed nations, sing and own,
> Your ransom was a Virgin's Son.

At the termination of each exercise sing, or recite thrice—

> Exert for us a Mother's care,
> And us thy children own;
> Prevail with Him to hear our pray'r
> Who chose to be Thy Son.

FIRST DAY.

ORIGIN AND PRACTICE OF THE MONTH OF MARY.

Love Mary, serve her, and Heaven will be yours.

JESUS hath found the secret of dwelling with His children even to the consummation of ages by the most admirable invention of His love. If it has been withheld from Mary to offer us a similar proof of love, does not her Divine Son appear to have indemnified her for it by those wonder-working gifts whereof He has, as it were, deprived Himself in her favour? Yes; Mary, it may be said, by those admirable and miraculous graces which she is pleased to shower down upon all, has rendered herself present to our faith—she really dwells in heart and affection with us. Then let us not seek her in Heaven only—it is too remote. She resides in her sanctuaries, where she so often makes herself felt in our souls; she leads us by the hand; she is near unto us wherever we invoke her—nay, more, she abides with Jesus in the depth of our hearts.

The Church, invariable in faith and doctrine, has nevertheless from age to age sanctioned many new practices, suggested by the Holy Spirit, according to her necessities, as means to lead her children to the haven of a blessed eternity. Mary, ever attentive to cooperate in the great work of the redemption of souls, has been pleased also to reanimate our faith and confidence in her protection, a means so sweet and powerful of salvation. Not a century but can boast some institution of this kind. What might we not say of the holy Scapular, the Rosary, the several pilgrimages to which miraculous events have given rise? How often has not this tender Mother appeared visibly to her servants? What ingenuities has she not employed to win back her very enemies to her Divine Son? And even in our own days does she not seem to surpass herself, as though she took occasion from our indifference and the weakness of our faith to multiply her prodigies? The Living Rosary, the miraculous medal, the Archconfraternity of Mary — are not these standing memorials of her love and watchful protection?

As to the Devotion of the Month of Mary, of which there is question at present, it was inspired by the Blessed Virgin herself to a fervent Italian Missionary of the last century. He chose the month of May, as being the fairest in the year, and consequently most worthy of being offered to Mary. It was the month when, with the return of spring, disorders became multiplied in Italy, and through this pious practice it became a month of benediction and salvation. From Rome, which had been its cradle, this Devotion spread rapidly through Italy, and thence through entire Europe. It was known in France towards the close of the reign of Louis XV., but remained for a long time confined to private oratories. It is only at present that it has become popular, and we may exult in the thought that there is hardly a parish in our cities, towns, or villages that does not render this tribute of love to Mary. Whole volumes would not suffice to relate the wonders of sanctification effected by this salutary practice.

But it may be asked, what conditions are required in order to participate in the graces so liberally bestowed on the invocation of Mary during these days of salvation? Let us premise that, among those who already know her, Mary seeks children who honour her in spirit and in truth. It will not, therefore, suffice to encircle her altars daily, to listen to her praises, to sing canticles in her honour. This is something; but we must, moreover, accompany these pious practices by the spirit of faith and interior recollection, which are the soul of them; we must propose to ourselves a special end in the devotions of the month—as to obtain a victory over some defect, the acquisition of some virtue, to ask through Mary herself grace to love her constantly, the conversion of some sinner, or any other favour we desire. Without some definite end we feel no ardour; we obtain nothing because we have asked nothing.

Practices for each day of the Month of Mary.— 1. To recite daily three times the appointed aspiration. 2. To perform two or three acts of mortification, or denial of your own will, in order to obtain the favour you solicit. 3. Every morning to place yourself under the protection of the Blessed Virgin, thinking with joy that this is the month to obtain all you ask, resolving to spend each day of this prolonged Feast, during which so many hearts honour her perfectly, under the eyes of Mary.

Aspiration.— "This is the day," this is the month, "that the Lord hath made" to honour His Mother; "let us be glad and rejoice therein" —*Hæc dies quam fecit Dominus, exultemus et lætemur in ea.*

First Day.

Example.

"My Mother is the attraction that brings souls to Me," said our Lord to St. Bridget. Each day verifies this word of the Divine Master. To the exercises of this month we are indebted for a conversion, which in our own days has proved no less startling to the world than consoling to the Faithful —that of the Carmelite Father, Augustine Mary of the Blessed Sacrament.

The offspring of Jewish parents, Hermann Cohen was born at Hamburg in 1821. He, at an early age, embraced the career of an artist, and, being attracted to Paris in 1834, became ere long one of the most distinguished pupils of Listz. Intoxicated with success, he plunged into the vortex of the world and its amusements. But though in the midst of the enjoyment dreamt of by many an artist, the heart of the young Hermann sought for happiness in vain; an undefinable disquietude and *ennui* pressed heavily on his life. This situation continued till the month of May, 1847. At that time choirs of amateurs assembled every evening for the Month of Mary in the church of St. Valère. They solicited Hermann to preside at the organ, and the young artist, solely inspired by love for his art and the desire to oblige, repaired to St. Valère, where from the first instant he found his heart moved. "When the moment came for Benediction," he related subsequently, "though in nowise disposed to kneel with the rest of the congregation, I felt interiorly an indescribable trouble. My soul, stunned and distracted by the tumult of the world, found itself once more, so to speak, and became aware that something took place within her to which she had been hitherto a stranger.

Without knowing it, or rather in despite of myself, I bowed down. Assisting there again on the following Friday, I felt exactly the same impressions, and the idea of becoming a Catholic suddenly flashed upon my mind.

"A few days after, I passed one morning by this same church. The bell tolled for Mass. I entered the church and assisted at the Holy Sacrifice immoveable and attentive. I heard one, two, three Masses without thinking of retiring, though what retained me I could not conceive. I returned home, but towards evening was involuntarily brought back to the same place, and again the bell invited me to enter. The Blessed Sacrament was exposed, and at the first glimpse of It I felt drawn to the very communion rails, where I fell on my knees. This time it cost me no effort to bow down at Benediction, and on rising up I felt a delicious calm in my whole being. Sleeping and waking, my thoughts the livelong night were on the Blessed Sacrament. I burned with impatience to assist at more Masses, and, in effect, from that time I heard several at St. Valère with a joy that absorbed all my faculties. Pressed by divine grace, I called on the Duchess de Ranzan, and begged her to direct me to some clergyman; she sent me to the Abbé Legrand."

It was at Ems, in Germany, that truth, whose first rays Hermann had hitherto only perceived, finally appeared to him in all its splendour.

"There," he says, "the ceremonies captivated my attention; but, by degrees, the prayers of the Holy Sacrifice, the singing, the consciousness of the presence of a Power at once superhuman and invisible, began to agitate, disquiet, and make me tremble. In a word, it pleased the divine grace to descend on me in all its force. At the Elevation I suddenly felt a very deluge of tears flow from my eyes, nor did it cease for some time. O blissful moment! O moment ever memorable for my soul's salvation! . . . Still, still doth my mind dwell on thy remembrance, with the many heavenly sensations thou broughtest me from on high. Even now do I invoke with ardour the omnipotent and merciful God, that the delightful memory of His beauty may remain eternally engraven in my heart. I remember to have wept in childhood, but never, oh, never, had I known such tears as these. Whilst they flowed I felt the most cutting remorse for my past life surging up from the depths of a heart lacerated by conscience. At once, and as it were by intuition, I spontaneously began to make an interior and rapid general confession of all my grievous faults to God. I beheld them there, confronting me in thousands—hideous, repulsive, revolting, meriting all the anger of a just Judge. And, nevertheless, a strange calm stole over my soul; I felt that the God of mercies would pardon me, would turn away His face from my iniquities, would compassionate my sincere contrition, my bitter grief, my earnest repentance. . . Yes; I felt that He forgave me, and in expiation accepted my firm purpose of loving Him above all things, and of being henceforth entirely converted. Leaving that church of Ems I was already a Christian."

Influenced by divine grace, Hermann returned to Paris. He was baptized in the church of our Lady of Sion on the 28th of August, 1847, the Feast of St. Augustine, whose name he was subsequently to take on assuming the Religious habit. He had prepared himself by serious study and a long retreat for holy Baptism. The Abbé Legrand, who had had the privilege of sowing the first seeds of truth in the soul of the young neophyte, crowned his work by pouring the regenerating waters on his head. Ten days after, on the 8th of September, the new Christian approached the Sacred Banquet for the first time, and received, amid the most unbounded transports of delight, this celestial nourishment, the object of his most ardent desires. The assistants were struck with the marvellous splendour and supernatural expression which were suddenly diffused over the features of the young communicant. He formed on the spot a resolution to devote himself to God in the Priesthood, but it was not till 1849 that his Religious vocation manifested itself. During a retreat which he made between the Feasts of the Ascension and Pentecost, an irresistible desire drew him to the Order of the discalced Carmelites. After having conquered many difficulties, and surmounted, with that invincible perseverance which is the sign of strong vocations, all the obstacles which God, in His impenetrable designs, never fails to raise in the way of all holy undertakings, the ardent neophyte could at last bid an everlasting farewell to the world, and change his name of Hermann for that of "Brother Augustine Mary of the Blessed Sacrament." On the 7th of October, 1850, he pronounced his vows in the convent of Agen, and a few months after was solemnly ordained Priest.

Father Augustine Mary has often exercised the function of preaching, and each time he has appeared in the pulpit has been successful in moving souls. It may be asked what is his secret for producing such results, for the humble

Religious appears to ignore the most simple resources of oratory. He relates the history of his soul without order or method; he lets his heart speak—nothing more; and his recital is throughout interwoven with affectionate aspirations to the sacred mystery, which is the special object of his devotion, the Blessed Sacrament. "Long have I sought for happiness," he says, "and sought it everywhere. I have found it at last, and I come to bring you tidings, that you too may find it in your turn." And then he goes on to express his astonishment how he, but yesterday a poor Jew, should now be inciting Christians to return to God, forgotten in worldly speculations and their accomplishment.

Let us hear Father Hermann rendering testimony to Mary, and join with him in blessing this Immaculate Mother—"Whatever steps I have happily taken in the way of Christ since my conversion, and they are great if viewed in the retrospect, I am greatly indebted to our common Mother; to this good and holy Virgin do I owe my progress, to this Refuge of Sinners whom I have daily invoked with fervour and confidence."*

* *Conversion of Hermann, the Pianist.* By J. B. G.; and *Messager de la Charité.* By G. Cadoudal.

SECOND DAY.

HOW WE ARE TO HONOUR MARY.

"Better is one day in thy courts, than a thousand in the tabernacles of sinners" (Psalm lxxxiii. 11).

WE must not confound devotion to Mary with those many practices of piety which we are free to adopt, or neglect. The Church, the pillar of truth, has established a special worship to honour Mary, a worship less sublime than that due to God, but superior to what we pay to the Saints; a worship necessary to salvation, according to the testimony of the Fathers and Doctors—not of an absolute necessity, Christ being the sole Mediator between God and man, but of a moral necessity originating in the Divine will alone. St. Bernard says—"God having inclosed the entire price of our redemption and the plenitude of all good in Mary's womb, we have neither hope, nor grace, nor salvation, but through her." St. Anselm dares to affirm that whoever is forsaken of Mary will inevitably perish. St. Epiphanius styles Mary the great propitiatory of the world. "Wherefore," asks St. Peter Damian, "would God secure the consent of Mary, previous to taking flesh in her womb? For two reasons—1st, That we might owe her a deep debt of gratitude; 2nd, To give us to understand that this most pure Virgin is the arbitratrix of the salvation of mankind." The intercession of the Mother of God is then, not only useful, but even necessary to salvation; to venerate her is indispensable; it honours God, Who regards as done to Himself the homage paid to His Mother.

Hence the Church is especially solicitous to inspire her children with a tender and solid devotion to the Mother of God. She is never wearied in praising her; she honours her special Feasts and all her mysteries; she establishes new titles, new solemnities, to commemorate the benefits received through her mediation; and it is worthy of remark that on the Feasts of the Incarnation of our Lord, His Circumcision, Presentation in the Temple, it is Mary she seems to honour even more particularly than her Divine Son, the Office of these days being consecrated to the praises of this august Queen. It is with her invocation all the Offices of the Church begin and end; sacred orators publicly appeal to her to pour down on their words that celestial dew which alone can fructify them. How many temples and cathedrals have been erected under her patronage? Not contented with these homages, the Church has consecrated a day each week, a month each year, to be more especially devoted to her veneration, and daily at the Holy Sacrifice is her memory recalled several times to the Faithful, and presented to God with the Blood and merits of the Divine Victim.

Let us enter with joy into the spirit of our holy Mother the Church, let us rejoice that she sets no limits to the honours rendered to Mary, and let us say—O holy Virgin! one day passed in your sanctuaries, consecrated to procure your glory, is worth ten thousand, is worth a century spent in the most exalted functions. *Melior est dies una in atriis tuis super millia.* It is infinitely sweeter, more advantageous, more honourable to be the last of your true servants, than to hold the first rank in the tabernacles of sinners, were they even the kings and masters of the universe. I have chosen to be an abject in the house of my God, rather than dwell in the tabernacles of sinners.*

Practice.—It is not sufficient for the honour of Mary to confess and communicate on her Festivals, you must also enter by meditation and prayer into the spirit of the mystery the Church celebrates, thus imitating this divine Mother, of whom the Gospel says, that after the birth of Christ—" Mary kept all these things in her heart."†

Aspiration.—I know not with what praises to extol thy dignity, because Whom the heavens could not contain, thou hast borne in thy womb, O Mary!

Example.

It is impossible to really love Jesus and not love His holy Mother; accordingly, devotion to Mary was the favourite devotion of Blessed Alphonsus Rodriguez, a Jesuit Lay-brother in the College of Majorca. Words fail to express his affection for this heavenly Queen; she was his Mother, but a celestial Mother whom he cherished in proportion to the ineffable perfection he discovered in her. He was ever devising new expedients to testify his filial devotedness; whenever he could obtain permission he fasted rigidly on Saturdays, and prepared himself for her Feasts by every species of mortification, which obedience alone prevented his carrying to excess. Never was his rosary out of his hands. He had composed several devout prayers to his amiable Mistress, she was constantly present to his mind, he asked nothing of God save

---

* Psalm lxxxiii. † St. Luke ii. 19.

through the intercession of Mary, and counselled others to adopt this holy practice. In the year 1652, Father Francis Collin, who has written the life of Blessed Alphonsus in Spanish, being on the point of leaving the College of Majorca, in which he had spent six years with the Saint, went into his chamber to make his adieu; he found the holy Brother so ravished in God that he could kiss his feet with veneration without his at first perceiving him. Alphonsus, returning to himself at this moment, and seeing a Priest in this posture, was filled with confusion, and a modest blush diffused itself over his countenance. Without giving him time to make any reflection, Father Collin said—"My Brother, I am going to set out, leave me a spiritual souvenir to remind me of the years we have passed together." The good old man replied without hesitation—"When you wish to obtain anything of God, ask it with confidence from the Blessed Virgin, and be sure you will obtain it."

THIRD DAY.

ANTIQUITY OF DEVOTION TO THE HOLY VIRGIN.

I believe in God the Father Almighty . . . and in Jesus Christ, . . . Who was conceived of the Holy Ghost and born of the Virgin Mary.

TO imagine that the honours decreed by the Church to the Mother of God is a devotion of recent date, as heretics assert, would be untrue. If the Gospel speaks but little of Mary, it is that all her praises, all her glory, all her titles to our veneration, are comprised in these words of the Angel—" Hail, full of grace, the Lord is with thee;" and in this fiat—"Be it done unto me according to thy word," fiat which raised Mary to the incomparable dignity of Mother of God, remaining still a virgin. It follows as a natural consequence of her dignity as Mother of God that we need not fear to raise her too high, since all have agreed that, with the exception of those titles due to the Divinity alone, nothing is too great when Mary is in question.

If in the primitive ages of Christianity neither altars nor temples were raised to Mary, it was because the Church, guided by the Holy Spirit, deemed it expedient to be tender of Pagan minds, at a time when faith in the Incarnation and Redemption was still weak, and when the precepts of the New Law were, so to say, in their infancy. But who would doubt the tender veneration, the respect of the Apostles, of St. John amongst others, for the Mother of God? And consider the place occupied by Mary in that succinct and decisive exposition of our faith, the Creed. "She is there mentioned with the Father, the Son, and Holy Ghost, not as a stranger, but as one bound to Them by the strictest and most indissoluble alliance: in quality of Daughter, Spouse, and Mother."* And what must not have been the homage and unbounded confidence of the primitive Faithful in Mary during the long years she dwelt among them after the Ascension of her Divine Son, loading them with favours and rendering them maternal services?

Since that time, tradition is unbroken. In the second century, St. Irenæus recognizes Mary as our advocate; Origen, in the third, calls her a celestial treasure. In the fourth century, St. Basil ordains in his liturgy, that the Deacon who precedes the Bishop should say aloud to the congregation—"Let us be mindful of our sovereign Lady, the most holy and Immaculate Virgin, Mother of God." St. Augustine, in his book on Virginity, presents her to Christians as their good Mother, and wishes that all entertain those sentiments of veneration, love, and confidence, which children experience towards a mother. Could our most ardent devotion bear any comparison to what we are told of the expectation of the Faithful, and their acclamations when the Council of Ephesus had solemnly anathematized Nestorius, and declared Mary to be Mother of God? This ardour, these cries, a thousand times re-echoed by an entire people—"Blessed be the great, the august, the glorious Mother of God," can they fail to find a response in the hearts of Mary's clients? St. Basil of Selucia (fifth century) teaches, that since the greatness of

* M'Carthy.

God is ineffable and incomprehensible, the excellence of her who bears to Him the most intimate relationship, that of Mother, must be confessed to surpass all that men can say or think. St. Peter Chrysologus, Archbishop of Ravenna, in the sixth century, says—"Heaven was affrighted at beholding the majesty of God; nevertheless, a Virgin receives Him in her womb, with so perfect dispositions, that in return for this abode, He willingly suffers her to exact of His clemency, peace for earth, glory for Heaven, life for the dead, and salvation for those that were lost." St. John Damascene (eighth century) declares that it injures the Son of God not to honour His Mother. He says that he fastens his soul to Mary's feet as to a secure anchor, dedicating and consecrating to her his mind, his soul, his body, his entire being. That luminary of the twelfth century, St. Bernard, surpasses himself when speaking of Mary; he confesses that when her praises are his theme, he is no longer his own master, and the day he cannot find time to extol her greatness, he retrenches from his sleep, "having nothing dearer, or more sweet after Jesus," he writes, "than to think of His Mother, the worthy object of our most tender affection." Albert the Great, the Angelic Doctor (who lived in the thirteenth century), tread in the steps of the holy Doctors, their predecessors. St. Bonaventure (thirteenth century) has so excelled in this devotion, that the mere perusal of his works suffices to inflame others with that fire which burned in his own heart. St. Antoninus (fifteenth century) styles Mary the polar star, ever visible in the horizon, to guide all who travel across the sea of life; he says she enlightens and guides us at all times, night and day, in calm and

Third Day.

tempest, in prosperity and adversity. It was to Mary's feet St. Bernardine came to repose after the fatigue of his apostolic labours. St. Francis Xavier (sixteenth century) commenced his sermons by the recital of the *Salve Regina*. The Saints near our own time, St. Francis Regis, St. Francis de Sales, St. Vincent de Paul, St. Alphonsus Liguori, were all eminent for devotion to Mary. The honours rendered to her at the present day are, therefore, no innovation. We cannot err in following guides so sure, conforming to what they taught and practised, authorized by the Church herself. Oh! how happy are they who persevere inviolably in Mary's service. Let us say, with St. Anselm—" To serve her is more glorious than to command the entire world."

Practice.—We may find Mary everywhere, everywhere invoke her; nevertheless, there are certain places in which she is pleased at being honoured, and in which she seems more ready to hear our petition; profit with holy eagerness of every opportunity of paying her your homage in these privileged oratories, or churches. For if on one side we must avoid superstitious devotion that some place in pilgrimages and forms of prayer, unaccompanied by any interior reform, on the other side, we ought to respect and fervently embrace those practices which are the more agreeable to God, as they spring from a more simple faith.

Aspiration.—*Quam dilecta tabernacula tua!* O Mary, how dear and delightful are your sanctuaries to your faithful servant! My heart will there invoke you, though it be not given me to be there in reality.

Example.

None of the Apostles, not even the well-beloved St. John, has told us anything of the impressions produced by the presence of this divine Princess, who surpassed all the daughters of Israel in beauty and gentleness. But St. Denis the Areopagite, having once beheld Mary while she yet sojourned on earth, was so enraptured, that at first he could not believe she was a simple creature. Writing to his master, the great St. Paul, he says—" I confess before the omnipotence of God, in presence of the clemency of my Saviour, and the glory of the majesty of the most holy Virgin Mother, that having been introduced by John into the godlike presence of the most high Virgin, I saw myself surrounded by a splendour so dazzling, and my soul was penetrated by so pure a light, and inundated by so sweet a perfume of virtue, that, stupefied in mind and body, I was unable to support so lively and profound emotion. My senses abandoned me, and the powers of my soul gave way at sight of majesty so incomparable. God, Who dwelt in the daughter of David, is my witness, that had I not been instructed by the Gospel that there is but one God, I should have taken her for a divinity, and I cannot conceive greater bliss even among the beatified in Heaven, than that which inebriated me during these fortunate moments, all unworthy as I am."

FOURTH DAY.

DEVOTION TO MARY IS THE MOST SURE PLEDGE OF PERSEVÊRANCE.

O Mary! " thy bands are healthful binding" (Eccles. vi. 31).

ONLY "he that shall persevere to the end shall be saved."* Unerring oracle pronounced by the lips of God Himself, a dread oracle, because of its uncertainty as regards us. How many souls, striving to lift the veil that shrouds futurity, are disquieted and troubled at the bare idea—"Who knows if I shall persevere to the end? who knows if I shall be saved, if my name be written in the book of life?" O the depth of the wisdom and of the knowledge of God! Terrible mystery, which has caused even the Saints to tremble, warned of their frailty by the startling downfall of those stars that fell from Heaven like lightning, of those men whose conversation had been in Heaven, and who were afterwards satisfied with husks of swine. Would you, Christian soul, convert this uncertainty of salvation into a sweet and consoling certainty; do you wish to render your vocation, your predestination, assured? Love Mary, persevere to the end in the service of Mary.

If an Angel descending from Heaven came amongst us to proclaim solemnly the names of those thousand-fold happy individuals who shall either persevere to the end, or repair by a holy and salutary penance the faults of their youth, what would our trembling and expectation be!

* St. Matt. x. 22.

What the transport of joy in those whose names had been pronounced—what the terror and despair of those whom the celestial messenger had not specified! Now, such an apparition might be delusive. Do you wish a more certain, an infallible revelation? Love Mary, implore her love till your last sigh. "My children," St. Philip Neri was accustomed to say to his penitents, "do you desire the gift of perseverance, be devoted to Mary." In effect, it is from neglecting to implore her aid so many fall and are lost. Blessed Alan, being one day assailed by violent temptations, was on the point of yielding and being lost, from neglecting to recommend himself to Mary; but in this imminent peril our Lady appeared to him, and striking him on the cheek, said—"Hadst thou invoked me, thou shouldst not have been in this danger." St. Germain was, then, right in styling Mary "the respiration of Christians;" for as the body cannot exist without breathing, so the soul cannot live without recurring to Mary, through whom it obtains and preserves grace. "Blessed is the man that heareth me," says the Queen of Heaven, "that watcheth daily at my gates, and waiteth at the door" of my mercy.* Yes, for such, Mary will obtain light and strength to forsake sin, to advance in the path of perfection; this is why, according to the beautiful expression of Innocent III., she is called *moon* during the night, *aurora* at daybreak, *sun* during the day—*moon* for him that is in the night of sin, to enlighten him on his pitiable state; *aurora*, that is to say, harbinger of the sun, for him who, already enlightened, needs strength to attain grace; *sun*, in fine, for him

---

* Prov. viii. 34.

who is already in a state of grace, that he may persevere therein.

O Mary, your devotion takes root only in the hearts of those who will persevere. *Radicavi in populo honorificato*—" I took root in an honourable people."* In other souls it is but transient. "Woe to whoever contemns this sun!" says St. Ambrose, meaning who neglects Mary. St. Francis Borgia justly questioned the perseverance of those who had not a special devotion to the Mother of God. Interrogating his Novices one day as to what Saint each particularly honoured, he perceived there were some among them wanting in devotion to the holy Virgin. He immediately warned the Master of Novices, charging him to keep an eye on those youths. The event justified the Saint's fears: every one of these Novices lost the grace of vocation. "Happy they who love you," said Blessed John Berchmans; "if I love Mary, I am sure to persevere, and I shall obtain of God all that I ask:" for which reason the holy youth was ever repeating, "I wish to love Mary." Let us conclude with the words of St. Bernard—"Christian man, whoever you may be, your life on earth is less a journey than a perilous voyage. Would you avoid shipwreck, fix your eyes constantly on this brilliant star, invoke Mary; in occasions of sin, amid the anguish of temptation, in doubt, in danger, call on Mary; let her name be ever in your heart to inspire confidence, ever on your lips to invoke it. Follow Mary, and you shall not stray; confide in her, and you shall not despair; upheld by her hand, you shall never fall; under her protection, you have nothing to fear; let her be your guide, you shall surely be

---

* Ecclus. xxiv. 16.

saved; in fine, let but Mary take on her your defence, and you shall infallibly attain beatitude. Do this, and you shall live."

Practice.—Perseverance; this grace which gives worth and merit to all others, this gratuitous grace which we can never deserve, is granted to those who ask it, says St. Augustine. Wherefore let no day pass without beseeching Mary to obtain it for you, and be assured you shall be heard.

Aspiration.—O Mary, perseverance of the just, forsake me not a moment, and I shall be saved!

Example.

That the Blessed Virgin would specially assist him had been the life-long petition of St. Alphonsus Ligouri. The following is the prayer he composed on this subject in his *Visits to the Blessed Sacrament*—" O Comfortress of the Afflicted, forsake me not at the moment of death! Obtain for me the grace to invoke you at that time more frequently, and let your sweet name and that of your Divine Son hover on my lips till my last sigh. Pardon, O my Queen, pardon my boldness, come yourself before I expire; come and console me with your holy presence. This grace you have bestowed on many of your servants; I also desire and hope for it. True, I am a sinner, I am unworthy of it; but I am your servant; I love you, and place unbounded confidence in you. O Mary! I expect you; refuse me not this consolation." Alphonsus was not mistaken in his expectation. The 31st of July, 1787, his illness momentarily increased, but his peace and serenity were unalterable. About two o'clock in the morning, whilst two of the Fathers assisted him, and he held in his hand a picture of the

Blessed Virgin, they perceived his countenance suddenly become radiant, and a sweet smile played about his mouth. Some minutes before seven, the same occurrence was repeated. One of his Religious bringing him a statue of our Lady, piously invited him to invoke her for a happy death. No sooner did he hear the sweet name of Mary, than the dying Prelate opened his eyes, and, gazing at the image, appeared again to hold mysterious converse with the Queen of Heaven.

The morrow was his last day on earth. Surrounded by his numerous children, his joy and his crown, he entered into his agony. He appeared less to struggle against death than to converse with God in a prolonged ecstasy. His person underwent no alteration, no contraction of the chest, no painful sigh; thus, his hands clasping a statue of Mary, he calmly expired precisely as the Angelus bell was rung, 1st August, 1787.*

* Rohrbacher.

FIFTH DAY.

MARY IS OUR MOTHER.

"Behold your Mother"—Ecce Mater tua (St. John xix. 27.)

THE most precious good we possess in the order of Nature, the gift of God transcending all human gifts—is it not that of a mother? A mother, is this heart, this soul, that lives more in her child than in herself, who loved it before it could return her love; who loves it for the pangs and tears it cost her; is not repulsed by the natural defects, nor even by the faults of her child. A mother! she is the most secure haven in the storms of life, the sweetest consolation in its bitterness. Would it not have seemed as though something were wanting to the Christian in the spiritual order, had not religion presented him a Mother's aid? He who framed the heart of man is too well acquainted with its movements not to attach it to Him by this link—the sweetest of all human ties. "I will draw thee with the cords of Adam, with the bands of love."* Jesus, Who took upon Him our nature to compel our love; Jesus, Who had already given us His Father, commanding us to call Him daily *our Father*. Jesus well knew the necessity of a Mother. And He has given us a Mother; He has given us to His own Mother, but under what circumstances? On the Cross, at death, at the moment when friends take pleasure in giving to those they love the most tender marks of friendship, their most precious gifts. Jesus, looking around Him, beholds His Mother standing immoveable,

* Osee xi. 4.

offering, for the salvation of mankind, the most painful sacrifice a mother could make. And as impressions received in grief are the most penetrating and most durable, He chose the moment when Mary's Heart was crushed with, and her maternal tenderness wound to, the highest pitch, to cast us into her Heart, and give her for our Mother. He says to all in the person of the Beloved Disciple, "Behold thy Mother," and to Mary, "Behold thy son." O fresh and incomprehensible pang! "Oh!" cries out St. Bernard, "what an exchange; John substituted for Jesus, the servant for the Lord, the disciple for the Master, the son of Zebedee for the Son of God, a mere mortal for the true God! O Mary, how comes it that your loving Heart is not transpierced by this word, seeing that even our adamantine hearts are rent by the sole remembrance?"

Could you ever forget, O Mary, the children of your sorrow? Alas! we entered your Heart by a wound that knows no healing. In effect, since Jesus, from the summit of the Cross, bequeathed us to Mary as her children, never did she forget the obligations imposed upon her by this legacy of her dying Son. We behold her ever occupied with our interests, ever in motion from Heaven to earth, from earth to Heaven; above, soliciting grace for her poor children; below, bestowing it on them continually. Let us, then, cry out with St. Anselm —"Precious hope, assured refuge, the Mother of my God is my Mother! Say, then, in all security, O my soul, I will exult, I will leap for joy, since, whatever judgment I merit, my sentence depends on my Brother and Mother."*

* St. Bonaventure.

Practice.—Children delight in being told they are worthy of their parents, that they resemble them. Let a similar sentiment animate you, child of Mary; endeavour so to retrace in you the virtues of your Mother, that none can doubt the links that bind you to her. A sweet and easy means of effecting this is, to ask yourself before each action—" How would Mary act, how pray, work, converse, study, suffer, &c., were she in my place?"

Aspiration.—Precious hope, assured refuge, the Mother of my God is my Mother—*Mater Dei est Mater mea.**

Example.

Victoria Fornari, born at Genoa in the year 1562, of noble and virtuous parents, was a child of benediction from her tenderest years. The pastimes of her infancy were prayer, retreat, and the study of the divine law. At the age of seventeen she married Angelo Strata, a Genoese noble, who far from opposing her in works of piety, gave her himself the example. When any one asked him why Victoria never appeared in worldly society, he was accustomed to reply—" My wife is good for nothing but praying and taking care of her family." God blessed their union with six children, four boys and two girls, each of whom she consecrated to the Blessed Virgin at the moment of its birth. Mary Victoria lost her husband at the age of twenty-five. Resigned, but inconsolable, she turned in her distress to the Comfortress of the Afflicted—" Holy Virgin," said she, bathed in tears. " Virgin all-compassionate, take these little ones that I present to you, adopt them as your children since

---

* St. Anselm.

they are fatherless ; so far as I am concerned they are orphans, since I am incapable of fulfilling the duties of a mother." This touching prayer was heard on the spot. The Blessed Virgin appeared to her and addressed her in these words, which the pious widow afterwards committed to writing by order of her confessor—" Victoria, my daughter, take courage, fear nothing, I will place both mother and children under my protection ; let me act, I will take special care of your household. Therefore banish all anxiety, live contented. I only ask you to trust to my bounty, and henceforth devote yourself exclusively to love God above all things."

The vision disappeared, but not so the consolation it imparted. Mary Victoria then made a vow of chastity and bound herself to a life of complete seclusion. Protected by the Blessed Virgin, and sustained by frequent Communion, she frustrated the temptations of the demon and the seductions of the world. Of her six children, one died at the age of ten, after a lingering illness borne with the most admirable patience. The remaining five embraced a Religious life, and arrived therein to eminent sanctity. In 1604, she herself having converted a house she had purchased in Genoa into a monastery, retired thither, with some companions who were resolved to lead a similar kind of life. The end of this new institute, which still exists, is to honour the Holy Virgin in the mystery of the Annunciation and to imitate the hidden life.

SIXTH DAY.

THE GREAT LOVE BORNE TO US BY MARY OUR MOTHER.

"Can a woman forget her infant, . . . yet will not I forget thee."
(Isaias xlix. 15.)

MATERNAL love is the most sublime degree of affection and devotedness that the human heart can conceive. Behold a mother! night and day what are her cares, her solicitude? how happy and tranquil she is with her child! what is her delight in seeing its faculties develope themselves? how she watches the first faint dawn of reason? Her child is to her the entire world; wherever it goes her eyes follow it, her heart and mind are bent on it. All that heretofore amused her, attracted her affections, has now lost its charm; the most painful sacrifices, the most complete subjection, have changed titles, and are become joys in favour of this beloved one. Rejoice then, ye children of Mary, for such in truth is the generous and tender love that fills this Mother's heart for you. Night and day she watches over you without intermission. Her Heart, like the Heart of Jesus, admits no joy or sadness of which you are not the object. She, too, watched your first glimmerings of reason to make you comprehend her love, and to ask for yours in return. Throughout this universe, so vast and so magnificent, she beholds but your souls, they form the sole objects of her solicitude; step by step she follows them to win them to her Divine Son, nor can anything discourage her, or make her flag in her pursuit. We dare to affirm, compared to Mary's love for one amongst us, be he just or sinner, the united love of all mothers for their children is but ice. Need this surprise us? We have seen the Saints spend and wear themselves out with apostolic labours for mankind, their brethren, urged on by the charity of Jesus Christ, which pressed them not to live for themselves alone; and Mary, she who drew of the immense charity of the Heart of Jesus more abundantly than all the elect united, would she do nothing for her children but what our thoughts can fathom? We should, then, believe her when she tells us— Should a mother forget her child, " yet will not I forget thee."

But all that, it may perchance be said, is but a pious supposition. Let us then proceed to evident and palpable proofs. "God so loved the world that He gave it His only Son;" and in like manner Mary, says St. Bonaventure, "so loved us that she gave us her only Son." The consent required of her in order to her becoming the Mother of God, involved also her consent to the painful and ignominious death to which her Divine Son was destined; and such was Mary's acquiescence, that she sanctioned it by her presence, and in default of executioners she herself, St. Anselm and St. Antoninus tell us, would have immolated Jesus, with even more generosity than Abraham, in order to fulfil the will of the Eternal Father and to save mankind, her adopted children. What other sentiment save love, powerful enough to determine her to such a sacrifice? After Mary, where then, O man, will you find a creature who loves you with affection so heroic, that gives you so incredible proofs thereof?

And having done so much for us, beholding us

covered with the Blood of her Son, with that Blood which cries for mercy, and is all-powerful to obtain it, would she not love us, would she make no account of our souls, would she feel indifferent to their eternal ruin? No, no, there is not a human being whom Mary does not love and protect. "Oh, how ingenious are the cares of this tender Mother for us! She opens to all the bosom of her compassion, she has desired the salvation of all, she has cooperated in the salvation of all."*

Let us give ear to our Mother's invitation. Thus she addresses us—My child, come to me when it is ill with you, when out of favour with men and with God; come, and I will reconcile you with yourself, your brethren, and my Divine Son—*Venias ad me cum tibi non fuerit bene.* Courage then, child of Mary; know that all who ambition this title she accepts and adopts. She thus spoke to one of her most devoted clients—"I am a Mother full of pity, and I receive with maternal tenderness all who desire, with fervour, to be my children, and the servants of my Lord; I shall always receive them with open arms, and shall be their advocate with the effusion of charity which the Divine Majesty has communicated to me." What happiness to be under the protection of such a Mother! Who shall ever dare to attack the children of Mary in her very arms? What passion, what temptation so furious as to vanquish them if they place their confidence in the protection of such a Mother?

We read in the *Revelations of St. Bridget*, that Mary one day said to this Saint—"If a mother saw her son under the sword of the enemy, think you she would not run forward to ward off the

* St. Antoninus.

stroke? It is thus I act towards my children, all sinful as they are, when they apply to me." "O Mary, tenderest of Mothers, behold then what you ask of us; it is that we call on you in all dangers, that we run to take refuge in your arms, crying out like little children, 'Mother, Mother!'"*

Practice.—Learn from St. Gertrude an easy practice to supply what is wanting in your devotion to Mary. This Saint, reciting at Compline the *Salve Regina*, lamented before God her negligence in Mary's service. It then occurred to her to offer with the recital of the *Salve* the Heart of Jesus to His divine Mother, to supply for what she should have done. Our Lord showed her that in virtue of this offering, His divine Heart repaired very amply all her negligences, and undertook to offer to the Heart of Mary all the homages she would wish to have rendered. And as the Saint was once reiterating this lament to Mary herself on the Feast of the Nativity, saying—"Ah! miserable that I am, my holy Mother, truly I am not worthy to praise you;" the most benign Virgin answered—"Your goodwill supplies for all, and especially this devout intention by which you are accustomed to offer me your prayers through the sweetest Heart of my Son, surpasses all you could wish to do in my honour."

Aspiration.—Could a child forget his mother—a Mother like you, O Mary?

Example.

Love this incomparable Mother how much soever you may, O children of Mary, still will her tenderness surpass yours. Love her like a

* St. Alphonsus Ligouri.

St. Stanislaus Kostka, who could not speak of his love for her without kindling a like flame in the hearts of his auditors ; who invented new titles by which to honour her ; who asked her blessing at the beginning of each action ; who prayed to her as if he beheld her visibly ; who was transported out of himself by simply hearing the *Salve Regina* sung ; who, being interrogated how he loved Mary, replied, "She is my Mother—what can I say more?" pronouncing these words with such emotion of voice and countenance as befitted an Angel sent down from Heaven to preach love of Mary, rather than a mere mortal. Love her as much as St. Philip Neri, who called Mary his delight ; as much as St. Bonaventure, who not only called her his Lady and Mother, but went so far as to name her his heart and his soul. Love her as well as St. Bernard, the great servant of Mary, who said to her—" Ravisher of hearts, have you not stolen my heart?" or as St. Bernardine of Sienna, who went daily to visit a devout image of her to express his love in tender colloquies. Love her as much as St. Aloysius Gonzaga, whose heart beat and cheeks coloured at the sole name of Mary ; or like a St. Francis Solano, whom love so far transported that he took a musical instrument and came to play and sing before her statue. Love her as much as Father Diego Martinez, S.J., whose singular devotion to Mary merited for him to be transported by Angels to Heaven on each of her Festivals, and be witness of the pomp with which those days are celebrated by the inhabitants of the heavenly Jerusalem, and who was wont to say—"Would that I had the hearts of all the Angels and Saints to love Mary as much as they love her. Would that I had at my disposal the lives of all mankind, in order to consecrate them to her service.' Love her, as did the son of St. Bridget, who used to say that nothing caused him more joy than to know how much Mary is loved by God, adding that there was no danger to which he would not willingly expose himself to prevent this Queen from losing one degree of greatness.

What shall I say further? Imagine all that love can devise to testify affection for the beloved; desire, with the Blessed Alphonsus Rodriguez, to give your life in pledge of your love; engrave on your breast with a sharp instrument the amiable name of Mary, as did a Francis Binance and a St. Radegunda, wife of King Clotaire; nay, stamp it with red hot iron like two of her servants, Baptist Arquenta and Augustine Spinosa, both of the Society of Jesus; in fine, exhaust all the inventions of love, never shall you attain to loving Mary as much as she loves you, and you must ever say, with St. Peter Damian—" So loving are you that it is impossible to surpass you in affection." It is related of the Blessed Alphonsus Rodriguez that, being one day prostrate before a statue of Mary, he cried out, in an effusion of tenderness— " My most amiable Mother, I know you love me, but you do not love me as much as I love you." Then the Blessed Virgin, regarding him with an offended air, replied—" What do you presume to say, Alphonsus? Oh, how much my love surpasses yours, there is less distance between Heaven and earth!"*

* St. Ligouri.

SEVENTH DAY.

THE CONFIDENCE WE OUGHT TO HAVE IN MARY.

"To whom shall we go?" if not to our Mother—Ad quem ibimus? (St. John vi. 69).

OF all the testimonies of honour and love we can bestow, the least doubtful, the least suspicious, is confidence. The heart of man, so imperfect, so weak, and consequently so vindictive, nevertheless allows itself to be disarmed by the confidence even of a foe; there is nothing we do not grant to one who relies on us. Confidence is man's tenderest, most sensitive point; the more noble and generous the heart, the more is this precious conquest desired. "Confidence," said an ancient author, "you are properly religion, and make its sacrifice." This confidence Mary makes the measure of her tenderness and gifts, and who has a better right to demand this tribute from our hearts? Of confidence in Mary we may say, as of the praises due to her—whatever extent we give it we can never carry it too far. Moreover, let us say it boldly, since we have the authority of Holy Church for the statement—devotion to Mary has this peculiarity, that it consists not principally in imitation, like that to others. Doubtless imitation is the complement and perfection of it, but what properly constitutes its essence, the condition without which it would cease to be, is confidence. O Holy Virgin! if devotion to you, the obtaining your succour, depended on copying your virtues, we should cease to love you, to be loved by you whenever we ceased to imitate you. And what would then become of poor sinners? To whom could they go when they had provoked the wrath of your Divine Son?

But on what must this confidence be grounded? Shall we trust in Mary because we serve her faithfully, because perchance we have been so fortunate as to burn with her love, to gain to her the hearts of our brethren? No, no; because these motives may be wanting to us, for our fidelity may have failed, may one day fail us. We shall trust, then, in Mary, because she alone, after God, can be called *good*, nay, goodness itself, because she loves us, because she is our Mother—and such a Mother must ever inspire confidence—because she is all-powerful, and, with her Divine Son, is alone able to extricate us from the most perilous, the most desperate, positions. We shall confide in her, for that we are weak, sinners, that a blast may overthrow us, and because this weakness, this impotency itself, gives us a claim to her compassion.

"But perhaps the dignity and sanctity of this Queen of Heaven affright us, make us apprehensive of recurring to her, miserable that we are, and defiled with sin."* "No, no; fear nothing; the holier she is, the more eminent her dignity, the more sweet and clement she shows herself towards the sinner desirous of being converted."† Ah! wherefore should a frail mortal fear to appear before this Queen of Mercy? Her countenance has nothing austere, nothing terrible; far from it, she shows herself replete with sweetness and bounty towards all."‡ Now, if Mary be so kind, so merciful to all mankind, even to the ungrateful and negligent, with what tenderness will she not regard

* St. Ligouri.   † St. Gregory.   ‡ St. Bernard.

those who love her, who frequently invoke her, who openly avow themselves her servants, and have in her unshaken confidence? "She is easily found by them that love her,"* and ever found overflowing with mercy and love. I love those that love me, she says; for though she tenderly loves all men as her children, yet for these who have a more special devotion, a more cordial confidence in her, she has a singular fondness. Hers is a discerning love, and she reserves her more signal favours for those who so confide in her as entirely to abandon themselves to her sweet protection and motherly solicitude. And wherefore should we not blindly confide to her own interests for time and for eternity, since she is our Mother? Ah! had a mother, like her, the will to heap gifts on her child, while at the same time she possessed the power to do so, what should be wanting to this fortunate babe? And shall not Mary do more for us than we hope for, does she not merit we should expect everthing at her hands, our own all-powerful Mother? Let us, then, cast all our solicitude into her bosom, trust to her the affair of our salvation, of our perfection, of our perseverance; let us not even ask any determinate favours of her liberality, but say with confidence to her Divine Son, "Lord, I ask neither consolation nor affliction, peace nor trial, health nor sickness; blind that I am, I might err in my choice; but what I desire, what I beg, what I beseech, is, that you will grant me whatever graces Mary asks in my behalf." And what more rational prayer could we frame, seeing that our Mother, Mary, desires far greater blessings for us than we could desire for ourselves; that the gratification she experiences in loading us

* Wisdom vi. 13.

Seventh Day. 41

with benefits is incomparably greater than our utmost longings to receive them. She even anticipates our desires, and is the first to show herself to the sinner, as the number of striking conversions effected so suddenly, so unexpectedly, testify.

To whom should we go, if not to our Mother? "Though she should kill me," says St. Bonaventure. "yet will I trust in her; full of confidence, I desire to die at the foot of her image, and I shall be saved."

Practice.—Live upon confidence in Mary. As a mother carries her infant, so will she bear you in her arms. Let this trust be so natural to you, that you will recommend to her your interests of each day and moment, as well the minor as the more weighty. Cast yourself completely on her care, and henceforward forego all disquietude, which is to the soul a waste of precious time.

Aspiration.—O Mary, when the enemies of my soul attack me in order to cover me with opprobium and confusion, I will reply—"I have hoped in the protection of my Mother, and shall not be confounded."*

Example.

A Polish nobleman, named Count Sckolinski, having been arrested in arms, during one of the recent stuggles of Poland against Russia, was condemned to death. At these terrible tidings, the Countess leading her son, a boy of ten years old, into her oratory, kneels with him before a picture of our Lady of Sorrows, to whom she addresses the following prayer—"Holy Virgin Mary, pray for us, protect us, save us, restore to a wife her husband,

* Psalm cxviii. 10.

to a son his father, you cannot but compassionate our tears; you who were never invoked in vain, who so fondly love your Divine Son, who have suffered so much yourself." Presently, Stanislaus and his mother arose. A secret hope has allayed their grief. Escorted by a domestic, and accompanied by her son, the Countess repairs to the prison in which her husband was confined. A few gold pieces slipped into the gaoler's hands gained her admission to his dungeon. Three quarters of an hour later, the unhappy Countess again passed the guards, her countenance concealed, and holding her weeping boy by the hand. It was evening ere the prisoner's cell was again visited. At the time of this inspection, the gaoler uttered loud cries, called for assistance and shouted "*treason.*" In place of the condemned, he had just found the Countess, his wife. Colonel Sckolinski had escaped with his son to Paris. A year and a half had passed over without the Count being able to learn the fate of his courageous wife. To the eager and repeated inquiry of Stanislaus—"When will mamma come?" he could give but a vague reply, dissimulating his own cruel uncertainty.

The boy had been placed at a Seminary presided over by ecclesiastics, and grew in learning, piety, and good sentiments. The period of his first Communion approached, and the idea of his mother haunted him unceasingly. "I wish," he was wont to say to his father, "I wish she may return for my first Communion, and she will return." Preoccupied with this desire, Stanislaus, one evening at study hour, wrote to Peter, the servant of the Countess, who had remained at Warsaw, the following letter —"Be kind enough to tell my mother, Peter, that I am to make my first Communion in a month, and that she must positively come to Paris to assist at it. I do not write to herself because all our letters are intercepted, but I depend on you to convey my desire to her.—Your fond STANISLAUS.—Tell mamma I am at school in St. D." This letter written, the boy slips into it a picture of the Blessed Virgin, the better to secure the success of his mission, folds, seals, and posts it. Alas! during this very proceeding, the Count Sckolinski received the following lines traced by an unknown hand— "No more hope—departing for Siberia—resignation. Peter is to make a last effort; but it is said the first attempt at evasion will be the Countess' death warrant. We love you, and pity you still more." Meanwhile, the first Communion was drawing nigh. Stanislaus had said nothing of his letter to his father or masters; he had spoken much about it to God; he had counted the days and the hours, and said to himself—" I will make a novena to the Blessed Virgin before my first Communion. I will so arrange that it shall conclude at the moment I shall receive absolution, and I will pray so hard, that the Blessed Virgin will be forced to restore my mother to us." It was the eve of the great day. According to a pious custom, the parents had been invited to the reception room, in order to give their blessing to their children. Among the rest came Count Sckolinski. Stanislaus flung himself into his arms; then kneeling, received the paternal benediction. "This is your blessing," he said; "but I hope to receive my mother's also." The father was silent. "Do you know mamma is about coming home?" he continued. "Ah!" sadly replied the Count. "I wish her," pursued Stanislaus, "to assist at my first Communion, and so she will. Do you see, papa, I have made a novena to the Blessed Virgin. It ends at five o'clock. I shall receive absolution at four; then I shall be pure as the Angels, and I will implore the Mother of God to restore to me my mother this evening, or at least to-morrow certainly." "We shall see," said the Count, attempting a smile; and not being able to continue the conversation, he took leave of his son.

At five o'clock that evening, Stanislaus directed his steps towards the porter's lodge, when he was accosted by one of the Priests of the establishment. "Where are you going, child?" "To see if any one has asked for me." "But your father was here this morning." "Ah, sir, I am looking for another visit; I expect mamma." "But your mother is not in Paris." "She is returning, I am sure." "Come, come, my child, I can conceive your wish and prayers; but no distraction this evening, my dear. The visiting hour is past; return to your companions." The novena was finished, and the child fancied that, in order to do the thing more perfectly, the Queen of Heaven was about to restore to him his mother immediately. Not to go to the lodge was a great sacrifice, but he made it generously. "After all," he said to himself, "my mother will ask for me when she arrives." Six o'clock struck, then seven, then eight; no one comes. Supper is over, and they are preparing to ascend to the dormitory. Stanislaus was a little discouraged. Meanwhile, a woman of neglected mein, her features drawn and emaciated, entered the lodge, and asked to see Stanislaus Sckolinski. The porter, mistrusting this late visit, plainly refused to call him. At length, weary of arguing, he consented to allow the Countess (for it was she) to approach the window, and look at the boys defiling in the yard. Stanislaus, who still reckoned on his mother's return, left the ranks a little, to cast a glance at the lodge. The mother had only time to cry "There he is," when she swooned away. How came the countess to arrive at the precise time specified by her boy? She had escaped from the hands of the escort that was conducting her into Siberia, and, flying towards France, reached Paris in disguise, without resources, without money. Where should she go in the vast city? Happily in his letter to Peter, Stanislaus had given the address of his school, and thus the Countess had gone straight to her son

EIGHTH DAY.

MARY IS QUEEN OF MERCY.

"Hail! holy Queen, Mother of Mercy"—Salve Regina, Mater misericordiæ.

WHO shall be able to count the mercies of the Lord, the effusions of His Heart on the miserable? They equal for each of us the moments we have to pass on earth; they extend without interruption from that eternity during which God loved us in His compassion, to that eternity in which He will crown us, as an ultimate pledge of this same mercy. But amongst all the mercies of the Lord, there is one we shall eternally sing, as the source of all the others—Mary, of whom Jesus is born; Mary, the Mother of Mercy.

St. Bernard asks himself why the Church styles Mary Queen of Mercy? "It is," replies he, "because she opens the abyss of divine mercy at will; so that no sinner, no matter what may be the enormity of his crimes, can perish if protected by Mary. She can do all she wishes in favour of her servants, and never suffers any one to go away from her dissatisfied at heart."

If Jesus is King of Kings, the Lord of Lords, then Mary, of whom He deigned to be born, is our Queen, our Sovereign Lady, for all the subjects of the Son are subjects of the Mother. But for the consolation of Christians be it said, Mary is a Queen full of sweetness and clemency, solely occupied in relieving the miseries of her subjects; and the Kingdom of God consisting of these two things, justice and mercy, the Lord has divided it into two parts: He has reserved justice for Himself, and has ceded that of mercy to Mary.* Let us, then, rejoice, since we have in Heaven a Mother so compassionate, so tender, whose function is to withdraw us from the divine justice. Should she ever seem unwilling to beg the Lord to avert from us the chastisement due to our offences, let us say to her boldly—"Think not, powerful Virgin, that it is wholly for your own honour and advantage you have been exalted to the dignity of Queen of the universe; but rather that, placed on the pinnacle of glory, you may intercede for mankind, your children and your brethren."

But is it necessary to address her thus, in order to incline that all-clement Queen to compassion? Long ere we solicited her has Mary prayed for us, has cast herself at the feet of her Son, saying to Him, even as Esther pleading for her nation— "My Lord and my God, if I have found favour in Your sight, if You love me, give me my people, for whom I prostrate myself before you; grant me the life of these sinners, for whom I implore You." Could God reject her petition? Every prayer that proceeds from her lips is a law accepted by the Lord, by which He obliges Himself to be merciful to those for whom she intercedes. For, if Mary owes her Son an infinite debt of gratitude for condescending to choose her for His Mother, it may with equal truth be said that Jesus Christ has vouchsafed to contract a kind of obligation towards His Mother in return for the humanity which He holds from her. Mary knows well how to assert her rights. St. Bridget heard our Lord one day say to His Mother, "Ask whatever you desire."

* Gerson.

To which Mary replied, "I ask You to show mercy to the miserable."

What should, then, be our confidence in Mary, since we behold at once her power with God and the extent of her compassion. No! there is not in this world a being who has not experienced her pity and partaken of her benefits. "I am," said the Blessed Virgin to St. Bridget, "the Queen of Heaven, the Mother of Mercy; I am the joy of the just, the gate through which sinners go to God. To none on earth is my pity denied, not a soul that has not obtained some grace through my intercession, were it only the being less violently tempted by the demon. No sinner," she adds, "is so rejected in this life by God, that he may not with my aid be restored to grace. Wherefore woe, everlasting woe, to him who, having it in his power to benefit by my commiseration, neglects it, and so is lost through his own fault."

Let us then go, Christians, let us go to this most clement Queen; let us press round her throne, whence salvation shall come to us; let not the view of our sins keep us at a distance; for if Mary has been crowned Queen of Mercy, it is in order that the greatest sinners may be saved through her protection. Let us say with St. Bernard—"Ah, Mother, have you not been appointed Queen of Mercy? Who are the subjects of mercy, if not the miserable? I, then, the most miserable of sinners, am the first of your subjects, and you ought to be more solicitous for me than for all others."

Practice.—Recite with increased attention those passages of the holy sacrifice of the Mass, and of your prayers, which are addressed to Mary: the words in the *Credo*, "Who was conceived of the

Virgin Mary;" in the *Confiteor*, "I confess to Blessed Mary ever Virgin;" in the *Angelus*, &c. This practice will, perhaps, appear trivial; but, poor that we are, what can we do great for such a Queen? Moreover, he who loves finds every expedient good that aids him to testify his affection; and in Mary's eyes, nothing done to please her is unvalued.

Aspiration.—O Queen of Mercy! you who will not the death of a sinner, but that he be converted and live, take pity on me.

Example.

A celebrated history is that of Mary of Egypt, which is related in the first volume of *Lives of the Fathers of the Desert*. At twelve years of age she forsook her paternal home and came to Alexandria, where her licentious life made her the scandal of the inhabitants. Sixteen years had she spent in crime and disorder, when caprice led her to join a band of pilgrims who were embarking for Jerusalem, whither they repaired to celebrate the Feast of the Exaltation of the Holy Cross. Arrived in that city, and the festival day being come, a feeling of pure curiosity led her to desire to enter the church with the crowd, but she felt herself thrust back by an invisible hand; thrice did she attempt to cross the threshold, but to no purpose. Then this miserable sinner, enlightened by Heaven, understood that it was her crimes closed against her the house of God. There was under the peristyle of the church an image of the Blessed Virgin, painted on the wall. Raising her eyes and perceiving it, she prostrated herself, and, melting into tears, she made interiorly this prayer—

"O Mother of my God, have pity on a wretched creature; you are the Refuge of Sinners, refuse me not the consolation to see and adore the sacred wood on which your Son, my Saviour, shed His Blood to redeem me. After this I promise you to go and weep over my sins the remainder of my days, in whatever place you will be pleased to appoint me." Feeling assured that the church would now be open to her, she presented herself, entered unimpeded with the others, and adored the Cross with the most lively sentiments of compunction. Then, returning to the picture, she thus addressed the Blessed Virgin—"O Mother of God and my protectress, behold me ready, whither will you have me go?" A voice replied, "Cross the Jordan, and you shall find the place of your rest." The sinner made a general confession of her whole life, received Holy Communion, then, having passed the river, she buried herself in the desert, which she understood to be the place of her penance.

During the first seventeen years which the holy penitent spent in solitude, she experienced continual assaults on the part of the enemy; in these violent tempests she did nothing but invoke Mary, and through her aid was always victorious. After these years of trial the struggle ended, and she had passed forty-seven years in the desert, when, by a disposition of His providence, God permitted the Abbot Zozimus to discover this hidden treasure. The holy solitary related her history to him, then prayed him to return the following year and bring her the Holy Eucharist. The Abbot consented, and was faithful to his word. Having received Holy Communion from his hands, Mary made him promise to return the next year on the same day.

Eighth Day. 51

Zozimus in effect came, but found her dead. Her body was surrounded by a brilliant light, and traced on the sand he beheld these words—"Bury here the body of the poor sinner Mary, and pray for the repose of her soul." Zozimus interred the body, with the aid of a lion, which came to hollow out the grave; and on his return to the monastery, he related the marvels of divine mercy towards this happy penitent.

NINTH DAY.

MARY IS THE CONSOLATION OF THE AFFLICTED.

Tribulations and sufferings have encompassed me on every side, and I have invoked the name of Mary.

BANISHED children of Eve, exiled from our native land, and compelled to wander in this valley of tears, how sad and downcast our soul sometimes feels. And if with the royal Prophet we interrogate it, and ask—" Why art thou sorrowful, O my soul, and why dost thou disturb me?" immediately each individual suffering of this soul presents itself to the mind: weariness, apprehensions, hopes deceived, subjection to the body, temptations, inconstancy, innumerable sins, graces abused, the uncertainty of salvation; the evils of the day; public calamities, domestic afflictions, loss of health, goods, relations, friends, honour, credit; our personal ills, the affliction of those of our brethren with whom we sympathize—is not all this sufficient to cast the soul into sadness? But in those moments, when all things in Heaven and on earth seem to fail her, when she finds herself without energy, without elasticity, without life, let her at least turn to Mary, let her still turn to the Comfortress of the Afflicted, let her say, in the words of Holy Church—" O Mary, to thee do we send up our sighs, mourning and weeping," she shall soon behold help coming to her from on high.

Oh, yes; make the experiment—" Is any of you sad? Let him pray."* Let him pray to Mary,

* St. James v. 13.

and *then* tell us whether he has not been comforted, even more promptly, more amply, than he could have ventured to anticipate; whether *he* cannot also cry out in the transports of his gratitude—" Tribulations and sufferings have encompassed me on every side, but I invoked the aid of Mary, and I was at once relieved." Because it is not simply that the Blessed Virgin runs to succour us, she flies, with speed surpassing that of the Seraphim, she is borne wherever the wail of any of her children rises up to her. "What," says St. Peter Damian, addressing Mary, " could it be that your elevation to the dignity of Queen of Heaven would cause you to forget the sad condition in which we languish? God forbid! On the contrary, if Mary's pity was great while she was yet exiled upon earth, greater far is it now that she reigns in Heaven, where she knows more perfectly the extent of our necessities." Justly, therefore, might Blosius cry out—" O Mary! who could help loving you? In darkness, in doubt, you are our light; our comfort in sadness, our refuge in danger. You are, after your Divine Son, the assured salvation of the Faithful. Hail, hope of the forlorn! hail, stay of those bereft of earthly support! hail, you to whom your Son has given such power, that whatever you will is forthwith accomplished."

The devout Lanspergius represents our Lord Himself as speaking thus—" Children of Adam, dwelling amid enemies, subject to manifold miseries, honour with special devotion My Mother and yours; I have given her to the world as an example, as an impregnable fortress, that she may be your asylum in the many tribulations by which you are encompassed. Let no one fear her, none dread to approach her, for I have created her so meek, so merciful, in order that she may despise none, that she may not refuse her services to any who beseech them, but rather that, opening the bosom of her compassion to all, she should allow no one to depart from her with an afflicted heart."

Take confidence, then, O my soul! "In the world you shall have distress"*—but Jesus, Mary, have overcome the world, and the bitter waters of tribulation shall never be able to extinguish charity in your heart, if you know how to recur to the tender Comfortress of the Afflicted.

Practice.—Mary does not come to our assistance in afflictions because we exhaust all human resources in a measure before we turn to her. Let her henceforth be our first refuge, and she will herself direct us in the employment of those human means to which on certain occasions we may and ought to have recourse.

Aspiration.—Comfortress of the Afflicted, take pity on your poor children.

Example.

At the time when the Turkish Sultan, Schin, having conquered the island of Cyprus, was equipping a formidable fleet in order to resist the Pope and Christendom, Uchiali, Dey of Algiers, a Calabrian renegade, going to join the army of the Grand Seignor, pillaged the Isle of Cerigo on his way. Among the inhabitants was a youthful widow of twenty, named Angelica Gaggioli, whose piety and good works were remarkable. She was the mother of three children, two boys, and a girl, aged six,

* St. John xvi. 33.

named Anne. When she saw the Turks on the point of forcing open her house, Angelica, without thinking of her wealth, ran to a picture of the Blessed Virgin, before which she was accustomed to pray with her children; she concealed it about her person fearing its profanation, trusting that Mary would be her safeguard in return. The infidels, however, carried away Angelica and her little ones. Uchiali gave orders that they should be well cared, and did everything possible for a man of his character towards softening their sad fate. The society of her three children was Angelica's only comfort; she used to secretly assemble them, show them the picture of the Blessed Virgin, make them pray before it, then in terms suitable to their years, she impressed upon them never to forget Jesus Christ and His Blessed Mother.

Uchiali having been created Grand Pacha of the sea, in requital of his services at the battle of Lepanto (1571), the prisoners he had captured were sold and dispersed, the children of Angelica among the number. Her two boys, of whom the elder was only five, fell to the lot of a corsair of Tripoli. She had the pain of witnessing the sale of her daughter to a merchant, formerly a Jew, now on his way to Algiers, whilst she was herself purchased by a Spanish renegade named Momi. The Blessed Virgin was her only refuge, and through her intercession God gave her truly supernatural strength. For a time Momi treated her with much kindness, hoping to induce her to abjure Christianity and marry him, but seeing all his pains superfluous, he put her in irons. She passed fourteen years, sometimes set at liberty by Momi, sometimes confined in dungeons, beholding the empaling or burning of some Christian, whom the barbarian took pleasure in torturing. At length Momi, wearied with Angelica's constancy, resolved to sell her again. Hearing that a neighbour of his, a merchant named Cato-Mahomet, sought a slave to care his little daughter, a child of two or three, he treated with him, and disposed of Angelica. When she was handed over to her new master, she had a confused idea of having seen him before. He brought her to his house and said to his wife—"Anne, here is a slave I have purchased for you, she will tend our little girl, and I have chosen a Christian, because persons of this religion bring up children much better than the women of this country."

During this discourse Angelica and the young woman, equally amazed, looked at each other with astonishment and a secret joy. Cato having departed, the mother and daughter soon recognized each other, and yielding together to the feelings of their hearts, both rushed forward to a mutual embrace; tears fell in abundance from their eyes, and, after a few moments of silence and bewilderment, Angelica related to her daughter by what means God had brought her under her roof. Anne in her turn told her how, having been brought up with invariable kindness by Cato, he had obliged her to marry him at the age of thirteen, that she had never had a child but the little girl she beheld, that she found herself compelled to profess Mahometanism, although she had not forgotten the instructions of her mother, and remained at heart a Christian—in fine, that she had always desired to find herself once again among those of her own faith and renounce that impious worship she had been constrained to adopt. Angelica consoled her, she inspired her with the hope that God and His holy Mother would vouchsafe to take care of them; and they agreed mutually not to discover their secret to Cato, but await patiently till Heaven would furnish them with an opportunity of escape.

One day Cato, speaking to his wife about Christians, said, "The obstinacy of this sect regarding belief in their creed is invincible. There is in the baths here a young slave scarcely seventeen or eighteen years of age, who during the last week has been bastinadoed three times, because he was surprised in the act of reciting some of his prayers; and notwithstanding this punishment, he has just now been detected in a repetition of the same act." Anne pretended to be angry with the slave, and begged her husband to show him to her. They went to the window, and she saw a young man stretched upon straw, who with clasped hands and eyes raised to Heaven, seemed to pronounce some words. "I wager," said Cato, "that he still repeats the same prayers; if such a slave belonged to me I would have him empaled on the spot." Anne and her mother judged they might confide in one who suffered with such constancy for Jesus Christ, so despatched a letter to him in these terms—" Christian, the courage you have displayed convinces us that you are well instructed in your religion, and that being faithful to God you will also be true to us. Reflect if there be one among your comrades on whom you can rely; we will forward whatever sum may be necessary for your ransom: on this condition, however, that you promise to exert yourself according to our directions in procuring the liberation of two Christian females. We await your answer. God bless you, Christian."

This letter was the source of much joy to the young slave. His reply was as follows—" May God preserve you in the sentiments which at present animate you, and may He reward you in your charity in my regard. I am equally impatient with you to behold myself once more among Christians, not so much to be freed from slavery as to obtain instruction in my faith, having been carried off by the infidels at the age of five. I can nevertheless assure you I am a Christian, though I know only one prayer, which is addressed to the Blessed Virgin, and was taught me by my mother. I frequently repeat it, therefore it is I experience the bad treatment of the Turks; but the Holy Virgin has enjoined me to continue faithful. I often see her in my dreams, and a short time since she told me I should soon be set at liberty. Doubtless it was you she had in view in speaking thus. I am ready to carry out all your orders and can swear for two Neapolitans and myself that we will sacrifice our lives to fulfil your designs." This reply sustained the hopes of Anne and Angelica, but it renewed the mother's grief—"This slave," she said, "lost his liberty at the age of five; my eldest boy was precisely that age when he was torn from my arms." "If it were he," rejoined Anne. "God is omnipotent, my daughter," she returned; "He has brought me to you, He can restore to me my elder boy, He can enable me to recover the second; but how many children of the same age have been carried off by these barbarians!"

In the meantime they found an opportunity to interrogate the slave: he answered that he had a very faint recollection of his parents, he remembered only that his name was Anthony, that he, his mother, sister, and a younger brother, had been carried away together; that his mother was accustomed to make them pray in common before a picture of the Blessed Virgin. "It is my son," cried Angelica; "he was named Anthony, he prayed with you before the picture I had brought with me. It is he, my heart tells me, I have no further doubt." The young slave informed them that he and his brother had been taken by a corsair from Tripoli, they had continued in his service till the present year; that this pirate having been attacked about three months since by a Neapolitan vessel, they had boarded each other, when his brother had thrown himself among the Christians, while he had been unable to do so, and the vessels ungrappling with mutual loss, his master's had put in at Algiers, where, renouncing his piratical career, he sold all his effects and slaves, among whom were the Neapolitans, of whom he had spoken, as well as himself. "God has restored me one son," said Angelica, when Anne had concluded the letter, "He will also send me the other. I dare hope it of His goodness, and the confidence with which He inspires me assures me thereof."

At this time the Bishop of Ampurias arriving with a view to treat about the redemption of captives, Anne narrated to him her history, had her little girl baptized, and gave him all the money requisite for the ransom of Anthony and the two Neapolitans. The latter agreed among themselves the measures they should adopt after their release, to arm a bark and carry off Anne and Angelica. Anthony learned then who were his benefactresses. Already had Angelica shown him the picture of the Blessed Virgin from a window; he had at once recognized it and placed himself on his kness to pray. Subsequently he received the following letter—"The time for dissimulation is passed, my son; it is not two strangers who rescue you from slavery, and who in return ask you for liberty ; it is your mother and sister ; the Bishop of Ampurias will tell you more on the subject. We are going with Cato to his country house, situated at a distance of three miles from this towards the west, about a mile from the sea. Let the Neapolitans remain in Algiers after their release, in order to keep a look out for you, and apprise us of your return. For you, my son, go and employ this gold, these jewels, to equip a vessel, then come and rescue us from the unhappy state in which we are. God and His holy Mother be your guides, my son ; think of our impatience and hasten to give life to her to whom you owe existence. Adieu."

Anthony was overjoyed on reading these lines. He and the two Neapolitans being set at liberty the next day, at once set out for Cato's country house, and spent some nights examining its situation ; they visited the roadstead, and took notice of a spot behind some rocks where they could effect a secret landing. It was arranged that the Neapolitans should remain at Algiers to give intelligence of Anthony's return to the Bishop. This last reached Naples in safety, and the Bishop having spoken favourably of him to the Viceroy, a frigate was placed at his disposal, which he armed without delay. Whilst the Bishop related to the Viceroy the adventures of Angelica and her family, he was interrupted by a nobleman, who said—"I greatly mistake or this Anthony's brother is one of my galley slaves. I commanded the ship that attacked the corsair, and amongst those who threw themselves on board my vessel was a youth who told me a part of what I now hear, but I regarded his recital as a tissue of falsehoods." The Viceroy commanded that the young man should be brought before him. The brothers being confronted, recognized each other and embraced. The Viceroy emancipated the slave, to whom Anthony imparted his design, and informed him of all that had occurred in Algiers. The frigate was equipped in less than a week; the crew consisted of forty men, accompanied by whom, the two brothers set sail for the purpose of delivering their mother and sister, an enterprize which, thanks to the two Neapolitans who had remained in Algiers, happily succeeded. The joy of Angelica can easily be imagined when she descried her second son among her liberators. She took the little Mary in her arms, nor did she forget the picture of the Blessed Virgin to which she owed so much happiness; in fine, they all reached the frigate, which soon receded from the shore. From Leghorn they proceeded to Rome, where they were welcomed by a vast concourse of people. They were presented to Sixtus V., who wished to receive in person Anne's abjuration. Cato, who had died most opportunely a little previous to her flight, left her a little son, who was baptized in St. Peter's, Cardinal de Joyeuse and Camilla Peretti, the Pope's sister, acting as sponsors. The little Mary having attained the age of sixteen, made her profession in the Third Order of St. Francis, in the monastery of St. Margaret beyond the Tiber, whither she carried the picture brought from Cerigo by Angelica and preserved by her during her captivity; it might still be seen there in 1767. Angelica, Anne, and her brothers lived and died true Christians, and left a striking example of the protection accorded by the Blessed Virgin to those who in danger place in her entire confidence.*

* Recueil, *d'Histoires Edifiantes*.

TENTH DAY.

TEN days have now elapsed since we entered on the Month of Mary; let us examine how we have spent them. Have we made them profitable? Let us thank God and His holy Mother. Have we anything to reproach ourselves with? Then let us redeem time lost, by the ardour of our faith, by our fidelity to the prescribed practices, by some courageous sacrifice. Regret for having been so slothful and tepid, at a time when so many hearts are so generous and fervent, will redouble our strength.

MARY IS THE REFUGE OF SINNERS.

"Sinners, the despairing, look upon Mary, and she will lead you into port" (St. Bonaventure).

DURING the days of His sojourn amongst us, Jesus, the Way, the Truth, and the Life, ever evinced a marked predilection for sinners. Tender compassion for those poor souls He had come to save shone in His every act and word, and that the effects of this immense charity, with which His Divine Heart was consumed, might be perpetuated through the course of succeeding ages, He imparted it to the Heart of Mary, whom He has given for our Mother, for a secure refuge against the effects of His own justice. Alas! from this distant region of forgetfulness of God your Saviour in which you have dwelt, who was to bring you back to Him, who effect your reconciliation? How could you dare appear, alone and unprotected, before the outraged God, had He not given His Mother for your support? Come, then, sinners, to this secure haven, to this inviolable asylum, to Mary. Sinners—and which of us is not included in the term—who is so blessed as never to have offended God? Come, then, all to Mary! Oh, what is not her solicitude when she beholds us suspended over the abyss! What efforts does she not make use of to snatch from eternal ruin ungrateful children, whom she loves, although they have forgotten her very name of "Mother"—perchance never known, never invoked it. "My Mother," said our Lord to St. Bridget, "is the gentle magnet with which I attract sinful souls." And, in effect, "If the sinner who prays is unworthy of being heard, the merits of Mary intercede for and save him."*

The sinner is Mary's child of predilection. Why? Because he has cost her more than others. She loves him as a mother loves the child of whom death threatens to deprive her—with the same anguish, the same agony of heart. She perceives that, without more efficacious help, a more persevering diligence, this child will be wrested from her. Menaced with his loss, her bosom yearns; she forgets all the wrongs he has inflicted on her, and seems to act, love, life for him alone.

"Have pity on me, Lord, Thou Son of David," said the Canaanean woman, whose faith Jesus extolled, "my daughter is grievously tormented by a devil." Why did she say, "Have pity on *me*," since it was the cure of her daughter, and not her own, she solicited? Ah! it was because a mother feels the sufferings of her children as if they were her own. It is thus Mary prays for the guilty soul. "Have mercy on me, my Lord," she says to God;

* St. Anselm.

"this poor erring one is my child. Have pity, then, on me; save her—she has already cost me much." "Lord," can she say again, with that woman whom Joab sent to David to soften him towards Absalom the fratricide, "I had two sons, Jesus and the sinner; the latter crucified my Jesus, and now Your justice would bereave me of the second by smiting the culprit."* Could the Lord be deaf to this prayer—He Who has committed sinners to Mary's guardianship, to be cared for as her children? What more consoling title than that of Refuge of Sinners, under which the Church teaches us to invoke her? Truly this Divine Mother is the city of refuge, in which the greatest sinners are sheltered from the pursuit of divine justice. "He Who is fortunate enough to enter this city needs no words to ensure his safety. Let us, then, hasten into this fortress, and there hold our peace. 'Let us enter into the fenced city and let us be silent there.'† If confusion for our faults seal our lips in presence of the Lord, Mary will speak, Mary will intercede for us."

The Saints and Fathers of the Church are unanimous in their endeavours to make sinners sensible of Mary's commiseration in their regard. St. Augustine styles her the sole hope of sinners; St. Ephrem, the safe port of the shipwrecked; and St. Bernard, who terms her the ladder of sinners—it being by her they ascend anew to God —says to her: "O Mary, who but would hope in you, seeing that you come to the relief of even the despondent themselves? No, I feel no doubt that, in having recourse to you, we shall obtain all. Wherefore let him who despairs of himself

---

* St. Ligouri.   † Jerem. viii. 14.

—even of God—never cease from hoping in you." O sinner! did you but know the place you occupy in Mary's Heart, how lovingly she holds out her arms to you, you would rush to her knees; with her aid, you would deem nothing impossible.

Mary appeared one day to St. Gertrude, with her mantle thrown back. Under this cloak a troup of wild beasts was sheltered—lions, tigers, bears, leopards, which Mary, far from driving away, welcomed, and stroked with her hand in a commiserating way. The Saint understood by that, how the greatest sinners, when they implore Mary's assistance, are rescued from eternal death. "No matter how numerous and grave the sins of him who turns to me," said Mary herself to St. Bridget, "I lose all remembrance of his guilt; I see but the intention which leads him to my feet, and disdain not to dress and heal his wounds, because I am called—as in effect I am—the Mother of Mercy."

To insure her protection, Mary requires but one thing: that the sinner invoke her. If subdued by some passion which renders him the slave of hell, he nevertheless recommends himself to the Holy Virgin, and begs her with confidence and perseverance to deliver him from sin, no doubt but this good Mother will extend her all-powerful arm to break his chains and lead him into the haven of salvation. But alas! poor sinners, perhaps—like Augustine—pressed by grace, you *fear* to be heard *too soon*. It may be that you dread being cured, preferring to peace of mind, whose delights are wholly unknown to you, the pleasure of self-gratification. Expose this new wound of your soul to Mary—the simple avowal will touch her heart. She knows your weakness, and her pity for it surpasses your utmost feelings of shame and despondency. She will change this lamentable disposition into a thirst after justice and holiness, the labours of which at present startle you. Unceasingly, and with desires still more ardent than those of Monica over her wandering son, she will present you to Jesus enshrined in her inmost Heart, like a dead body in its coffin, to the end that this Divine Son may say to you also—"I say to thee, Arise;" and thus, after having restored to you speech and life by the power of His omnipotent voice, He may restore to His Mother this son that was lost.*

Practice.—To wear constantly either the holy scapular or a medal of the Blessed Virgin, as an abiding testimony of our confidence in her. Oh, how many conversions, how many graces, have resulted from this practice, at once so simple and so easy! How many persons has it preserved from imminent perils!

Aspiration.—O Mary! I am a sinner; nevertheless, say but the word, cast but a glance on me, and my soul shall be healed.†

Example.

Monsieur de Quériolet, no less celebrated for the scandals of his life than for the penance to which he condemned himself in reparation thereof, was one of the most glorious conquests of the Mother of Mercy. Enslaved to vice from his very childhood, his heart was proof against the Christian maxims which his parents sought to instil into it. Full of aversion for their lessons, he asked to be sent to Rennes, under pretext of pursuing his studies, but

---

* St. Augustine, *Conf.*, bk. vi. † St. Matt. viii. 8.

in reality to enjoy his liberty. There he associated with the most depraved students, resorted with them to the theatres and haunts of vice, persecuted to the utmost all the virtuous pupils, and, in order to secure accomplices, steals all the money he can lay hold on. Though his family had carried indulgence so far as to defray his debts, yet, on returning home, he purloined from his father's desk the sum of two thousand francs. Caught in the fact, and no less exasperated than confused at his exposure, he undertook a journey of six hundred leagues to gain the Turkish frontier, with the design of becoming a Mahometan. A merciful Providence placed a thousand obstacles to this sacrilegious design. After having wandered for a long time, Quériolet returned to his native country, in which he was a scourge by his quarrelsome disposition and violent deeds. A greater foe even of God than man, the threats of Heaven, far from inspiring him with a salutary dread, served but to inflame his impiety. "One day" (it is himself that speaks), "one day, as I was returning home from Rennes, the flashes of lightning were so continued and the peals of thunder so stunning, that I could with difficulty hold in my horse. Scarcely had I entered my house than a tree, struck by a thunderbolt, falls behind me. Vomiting a thousand imprecations, I ascended to my chamber and ordered my arms to be brought to me. I loaded my pistols, and opening my window I fired against heaven; proud of this achievement as of a victory, I went to bed. I was sleeping profoundly, when suddenly the lightning struck my apartments and burned one of the posts of my bed."

This sinner remained insensible to these signal marks of the Almighty's patience. A dream made

more impression on him. God caused him to
descend alive into hell, by a representation so
clear and vivid that, during the five or six hours
it lasted, it was impossible for him to turn away
his thoughts. He seemed to see the place that his
crimes had prepared for him in the depth of the
abyss. Fear got the better of him; he struck his
breast, did penance, and even entered among the
Chartreux. His passions were only lulled; they
soon awoke again. He secretly scaled the walls of
the cloister, and plunged headlong into every sort
of crime with greater eagerness than ever. He was
possessed by an infernal rage against everything
connected with religion — the Sacraments, the
Offices of the Church, its ministers. He blas-
phemed when the poor asked alms for the love of
God, and sometimes gave them something provided they would not utter that holy name. Yet,
despite so many excesses, through a lingering
attachment to the Blessed Virgin imbibed from
his virtuous mother, he never passed a day without
reciting the Angelical Salutation; it was to this
trivial homage rendered to Mary that he owed his
conversion. His parents had long and fervently
prayed for this, and had had Mass celebrated in a
chapel consecrated to the Mother of God, under
the invocation of our Lady of Mercy, for this
prodigal son, nor were their prayers in vain.

In 1636 he came to Loudon; curiosity led him
to the church at the moment the exorcisms were
performed. The demon descried him in the crowd,
and cried out by the mouth of the possessed—
"Behold my brave fellow, there's my fine fellow."
Then, addressing him, he said, in a vexed tone—
"What are you doing here? Why do you not go
away?" The spirit of darkness feared what was

speedily to happen. Quériolet, astonished, retired. The following day he reappeared in the church. The exorcist was then asking the demon why he had entered into the possessed—why he would not leave her. "How do you know?" replied the devil; "it may be for the conversion of this man." Saying this he pointed to Monsieur de Quériolet. The latter in his turn ventured to interrogate the fiend on some of the more hidden particulars of his life. He wished to know, amongst others, who had preserved him from the lightning when it struck his bed, and what was the cause of his leaving the Chartreux. To the first question the demon replied—"I should have carried you off, were it not for the Virgin Mary and the Cherub your guardian." To the second he answered, after much entreaty, that it was for certain faults which he specified, "God not being able to suffer so impure a man in a house so holy."

"Then it was," says M. de Quériolet, "I became alarmed; I felt myself completely overthrown, something inexplicable was taking place within me. On one side I felt myself urged to change my life, and to confess on the spot; on the other, I was withheld by a false shame—"What will they say if I confess, if I am converted?" Finally, grace triumphed. The new penitent, with tears streaming from his eyes, began to make aloud the avowal of his most enormous sins. In the course of the day he made a circumstantial confession of them, and found himself changed into a new man. Returning on the morning to where the exorcism was going on. "Hold!" cried the devil to the exorcist, "Behold your gentleman of yesterday. He is now in such a state, that if he persevere, he will be as high in Heaven as he would have been low down in hell with us." To whom is he indebted, after God, for his salvation? "The Virgin—she has put her arms up to the elbows in filth in her endeavours to withdraw him from his sinful habits." Who has finally brought him back to God? "Mary, this gentleman's great friend." Then eyeing him he said—"Your measure was filled up, but a spark of devotion to her still lived in you." Again, addressing Quériolet, the demon said—" Did you even lay down your life for her, never could you make a return for all she has done for you." After this, he cried out several times—"Ah! miserable that I am, if ever a change affected me it is that. I administered poison to him, which is sin, and now I am forced to swallow it myself. Wondrous change, to make of a man black as a devil a very deity. And I shall remain for ever miserable. Let me no longer hear of converting sinners, but rather of perverting souls."

M. Quériolet was thirty-four at the period of his return to God. His conversion was solid, and his penance was no less striking than his scandal had been notorious. That man, so haughty and brutal, was seen of a sudden to soften the violence of his disposition, to repress the fire of his passions, and give himself up to the practice of incredible austerities. His castle became a hospital, always open to the poor, whom he served with his own hands, with an incomparable humility and charity. He fasted for several years on bread and water; often passed two and three days without taking any food. His residence was situated a league from St. Anne, a celebrated pilgrimage near Auray. He went there frequently, and invariably went through the prescribed exercises of the pilgrimage, dragging himself along on his knees. In short, his penance was only equalled by his gratitude to Mary. Worn out with sufferings and austerities, he wished to breathe his last sigh in the Carmelite monastery of St. Anne. His body reposes at the foot of the high altar, consecrated to the mother of the purest of Virgins, of her whom the Church styles the " Refuge of Sinners," the " hope of the departed."

ELEVENTH DAY.

MARY AIDS THOSE WHO INVOKE HER IN TEMPTATION.

"Thou shalt arise" O Mary, "and have mercy on Sion: for it is time to have mercy on it, for the time is come" (Psalm ci. 14).

MAN'S life here below is one unending struggle —*Militia est vita hominis super terram.** As the fire proves iron, so temptation tries the just man. It is a necessary trial, a crucible in which is formed the valiant soldier of Jesus Christ, the soul is instructed, perfected, purified. "He that hath not been tried, what manner of things doth he know?"† Let it sink deep into our minds; the vivacity of our faith, the ardour of our devotion, may, indeed, redouble our energy in the combat, but they cannot shield us from the attacks of the enemy. Jesus Christ has said—"I came not to bring peace, but the sword." Model and Chief of the predestined, He would be tempted Himself, to serve as an example; and from Heaven, to which we are given a spectacle during this grand life struggle, He addresses us in these encouraging words—"For you, my saints, who shall have generously fought throughout your period of mortality, I will Myself be your reward exceeding great."

The devil, the world, and ourselves, such are the enemies we have to repel. Were we single-handed in the combat, it would be too unequal, but God Himself fights with us. "There is none other that

* Job vii. 1. † Ecclus. xxxiv. 11.

fighteth for us but our God." Moreover, He has given us His Saints and Angels for auxiliaries, and above all, Mary, His august Mother and ours. Oh, how prompt is she to succour those who call on her in the hour of peril! How skilful is she in discovering, in averting, dangers imperceptible even to ourselves! How many souls has she preserved in dangerous occasions, who shall never fully realize their obligations towards her, till the great day of eternity!

Life has its gloomy, painful hours; the soul is at times so violently agitated, so powerfully solicited, carried away, that there appears but a single step between her and the abyss of all disorder. Moments there are when her poverty, misery, incapacity for good, the wrath and indignation of the Lord, are displayed in so sombre colours, that she can cry out with the Prophet Jeremias—"He hath led me by dark paths, far away from that ravishing light which formerly guided my course. He hath led me, and brought me into darkness, and not into light. Yea, and when I cry and entreat, He hath shut out my prayer. . . . He hath shut up my way with square stones, He hath turned my paths upside down."*

O poor soul, in this bitter grief call upon Mary, cry, and desist not till she come to your assistance; not long shall you be obliged to wait. Let none give way to vain alarm, let none suffer himself to be disturbed; let us boldly encounter the enemy of our souls, let us oppose to him the name, the Heart of our Mother. "You come to me," let us say, with all the wiles of hell; I come to you in the name of Mary, which you would fain obliterate

* Lamentations, iii.

from the earth ; I come that all may know that this name is all-powerful in saving souls—*Tu venis ad me cum gladio et hastâ et clypeo : ego autem venio ad te in nomine Domini."**

St. Epiphanius says that Mary's compassionate eyes are ever looking down upon us, and seem to multiply themselves to discover our wants. "The Lord," says the royal Prophet, "has His eyes upon the just."† But your eyes, O Mary, are upon the just and sinners, like a tender mother who watches her child to prevent his falling, and watches also to raise it when it does fall.‡

It is, therefore, impossible that a true servant of Mary should perish in the combat—this divine Mother, covering him with the powerful shield of her protection, against which all the shafts of the enemy are blunted. Should the world present its pomps, its feasts, its happiness of a day ; should the devil stir up all the passions in his heart ; should the wind of inconstancy and human instability coming to shake him, represent this perpetual struggle as the rudest of trials, Mary will whisper to his heart, "My child, why keep your eyes fixed upon the earth. Look up, I beseech you, look up to Heaven, where light and momentary tribulation is rewarded with an immense weight of glory. *Peto, nate, ut aspicias ad cœlum.*§ Remember that a thousand years before God in the splendours of eternity are but as yesterday, that is already passed, so fleeting shall be their duration. And what will it profit you to gain the whole world, if you lose your soul? Will this wealth, these pleasures, these honours

---

* 1 Kings xvii. 45. † Psalm xxxi. 16.
‡ Richard of St. Laurence. § 2 Mac. vii. 28.

which dazzle you, be of sufficient value to redeem it?"

Practice.—Our Lord says in the Gospel, that He is never left alone by His Father—*Non reliquit na solum.** Faithful soul, child of Mary, exiled upon earth, ask your Mother to grant you the same favour—never to leave you alone amidst the foes sworn to your destruction. Incessantly call her to your side, by the groans of your heart. Oh, how sweet, how delightful is the company of Mary! How amiable and delightful will solitude appear with her! This solitude, in which the soul communes with Jesus and Mary, may be established in your heart, even amid the society, the tumult of the world; this is the admirable secret which Mary imparts to all who love her.

Aspiration.—Mary, Mother mine, leave me not here alone!

Example.

Blessed Alphonsus Rodriguez, being assailed by a fearful temptation to despair, had recourse to the recital of the Rosary. To render this weapon more effectual, he added to each "Holy Mary, Mother of God," this supplication—"Remember me." The combat waxing hotter and hotter, Alphonsus, pressed by his enemy, cried, in loud and energetic tones—"O my Mother, remember me; come to my assistance, I perish." Mary forthwith appears, and the storm is appeased. The devil one day put it into his head that all his efforts for the acquisition of merits were loss of time, since they would all end in a fall so great, that it would scandalize all whom his example had

---

* St. John viii. 29.

hitherto edified. The impression made by the spirit of darkness on the imagination of Alphonsus was so vivid, that the thing appeared unquestionable. His anguish is not to be expressed, but he invoked Mary, and she appearing, said lovingly—"Alphonsus, my dear child, where I am you have nought to fear." Once, when the holy man was grievously tormented in body and mind, a troop of demons appeared to him in the most monstrous forms, and after having insulted him in a thousand ways, they asked him, with infernal irony—"Where is your Mary?" Mary did not desert her Alphonsus. She displayed herself in the fulness of her glory; the demons, confounded, fled precipitately. Finally, in another vision, Mary condescended to say to her happy servant—"How I love you, Alphonsus!" Even this was not enough; she wished to manifest herself to him in a still more admirable manner. Whilst Alphonsus was reciting his Rosary, he beheld Mary descend from Heaven, accompanied by her Divine Son; and both took possession of his heart. For twelve years he entertained these amiable guests, nor did they ever after depart from him.

The demons who had persecuted him with such animosity during life, redoubled their efforts during his last illness. A grievous temptation to distrust assailed him, and, simultaneously, the most afflicting state of spiritual dryness and aridity. No more relish for prayer, no more heavenly consolations, no more holy thoughts. He forgot all the prayers he had been accustomed to recite, even the Lord's Prayer. In this dereliction, finding nowhere rest or alleviation, he could hardly breathe a sigh to Heaven, and such was his anguish of mind, that in comparison all corporal pains were as nothing.

Eleventh Day.

For five entire months the holy Religious continued a prey to this species of torture, more cruel than death itself. A calm at last succeeded this prolonged tempest; Jesus and Mary appeared to him, surrounded with light; conversed long with him, and having given him the most tender marks of affection, exhorted him to persevere on the cross to the end, warning him that nothing but sufferings remained for him here below. But from this period his trials were not devoid of comfort; scarcely did he invoke Jesus and Mary, than they appeared at his sides, and the graces they bestowed upon him were proportioned to his bodily sufferings, which continually increased. The demons dared no longer to approach him, after the Queen of Heaven had, in one of her apparitions, commanded them, with an air of authority, no longer to disturb her servant.*

* *Life of Blessed Alphonsus Rodriguez.*

TWELFTH DAY.

MARY IS THE TERROR OF DEMONS.

O Mary, to the enemy of souls " thou art terrible as an army in battle array" (Cant. vi. 3).

THE plot formed against the soul of each of us is worked out by foes so skilled in war, so crafty, so indefatigable, that were we fully cognizant of the perils that beset us, the mere idea would fill us with terror. Hence the Apostle bids us—" Be sober, brethren, and watch, because your adversary the devil goeth about like a roaring lion, seeking whom he may devour."*

We have, however, in Mary an assured protection against this enemy of our souls; from the beginning of the world she was destined to crush him—" She shall crush thy head."† And St. Bernardine of Sienna styles her the mistress and ruler of devils. To them she is more terrible than the sight of an army in battle array to one unarmed. "As wax melts before the fire," says St. Bonaventure, "so these wicked spirits remain powerless against the soul in which they find a frequent remembrance of Mary's name; the pious invocation of her aid; the imitation of her virtues."

" At the name of Mary, as at that of Jesus, every knee bends, even in hell itself; and not only the demons tremble, but they are filled with terror."‡ " At this name, which is for them like a clap of thunder, a flash of lightning, they fly, they are

---

* 1 St. Peter v. 8. † Gen. iii. 15. ‡ St. Bernard.

overthrown."* We learn from the *Revelations of St. Bridget*—"Such is the empire of Mary over the evil spirits, that whenever they dare to attack a soul who implores the assistance of this divine Mother, at her slightest motion they flee away trembling, preferring redoubled torments in hell to the experience of her authority."

Thus, if people would desist from the invocation of Mary, this wily enemy of souls would consent to cease in his attacks, confident, that once inveigled into this most dangerous of all snares, they would prove an easy prey to every other delusion ; he had the effrontery to say to Blessed Alphonsus Alvarez—" Cease to honour Mary, and I will leave off tempting you." A single glance at the image of this Mother of Mercy suffices to deprive the devil of all his strength and power. Interrogated once by a good solitary, concerning the continuance of the temptation that he had overwhelmed him with, Satan replied—" The torments I cause you are nothing in comparison with those you inflict on me. Swear secresy to me, and I will tell you what you must omit, that I may leave you alone." The solitary having done so, " I desire you," said the Evil One, " to desist from looking at the picture in your cell." This was a picture of Mary, before which he was accustomed to pray, and which he venerated from that time still more.

Mary is that Tower of David whereon a thousand bucklers are suspended with the arms of the most valiant. "As the Tower of David, a thousand bucklers hang upon it, all the armour of valiant men."† Poor souls! of what are you thinking

---

* Thomas à Kempis. † Cant. iv. 4.

when you withdraw from this impregnable fortress, when you permit devotion to Mary to become weak, when you neglect to invoke her in peril, lay aside her livery, abandon your pious practices in her honour! Ah! return to the combat, resume your weapons, at once so sweet and powerful—the thought, the name, the invocation of Mary; "for even the most hardened sinner does not call on her in vain; so much so, that if he continued pronouncing this formidable name the demon would be obliged to abandon his soul."* How easy would salvation become did we employ against our foes so sweet and assured a resource. Ah! let us not prepare for ourselves a share in the eternal, irremediable, regret which tortures the damned, that we could so readily have saved our souls through the name, the invocation of Mary, yet neglected to adopt this means so powerful in itself, so easily attained by all.

Practice.—There are three degrees in temptation —*suggestion*, or the thought of evil; *delectation*, or the pleasure that thought excites; *consent* or adhesion, by which alone the crime is consummated. Do you desire to vanquish the enemy, wait not till he has made some progress in your soul, but rather fly to Mary on his very first attack.

Aspiration.—"O Mother of desolate orphans, hear the cries of your children; spread out your wings that we may fly beneath their shelter from the face of the enemy."†

Example.

When St. Dominic was preaching at Carcassonne, they brought to him an Albigensian heretic,

---

* St. Bridget.   † St. Augustine, *Sol.*

whom the devil had taken possession of, in consequence of his having publicly cried down the Devotion of the Rosary. The Saint on the part of God commanded the devils to declare if what he preached concerning the Rosary was true, they cried out with terrific howlings—"Hear ye, Christians, all that this man, who is our enemy, has said of Mary and the holy Rosary is perfectly true." They added, "Mary, Mother of God, is our capital enemy; she upsets our plans, baffles our measures; but for her we should have overthrown the Church a thousand times by heresies and schisms." They then avowed they had no power over Mary's servants, and that there were many who, despite their demerits, were saved at the point of death by invoking Mary. They concluded by saying—"We are forced to declare that no one is damned who perseveres in devotion to Mary and the holy Rosary;" because Mary obtains for the sinners among them true repentance before death. St. Dominic made the people recite the Rosary, and at each "Hail Mary," several demons were seen to go forth from the body of the unfortunate man, under the appearance of burning coals. By the conclusion of the Rosary he was entirely freed from them. A vast number of heretics, witnesses of this miracle, abjured their errors and were converted. Even in our own days the virtue of exorcisms wrings similar avowals from Satan. Being recently interrogated in the person of one possessed, as to what we should believe concerning Mary, he replied—"She is a woman who has a Son; this Son is God; this woman was conceived without sin." Is she powerful? "She can do everything with her Son. Whoever has confidence in this woman is assured of salvation." She is, then, very compassionate towards men and sinners? "Oh, yes! she is merciful to all, ... except the devils." Thus it is that the force of truth sometimes compels the father of lies himself to speak for our instruction and consolation, even against his own interests.

THIRTEENTH DAY.

MARY IS OUR MEDIATION.

"*My only hope is in Jesus, and after Jesus in Mary*" (Euthymius).

BETWEEN the thrice holy God and sinful man what a distance intervened! Full of compassion for His weak creatures, God has destined to fill this infinite space; He has disposed in our hearts admirable steps by which we may ascend from this valley of tears to our heavenly home. It is through Jesus, through Mary, that we return to the God Whom we have so frequently deserved to lose.

The Second Person of the Adorable Trinity, the Word, deigned to assume our nature, to become man, mortal and miserable like ourselves; He united in Himself greatness and lowliness; showed Himself so powerful that all nature obeyed Him, so amiable and condescending that He drew all hearts to Him. And yet what a distance between man the sinner and this Man-God; between man, who despised the benefit of redemption, and the Redeemer! How shall he dare approach this God, so much the more irritated as He has the more profoundly abased Himself to prove His love? But let us not lose the hope of recovering grace, let us have recourse to Mary; it is she leads to Jesus, it is she who recommends us to her Divine Son, who reconciles us to Him, and puts us in a condition to be presented to His Father. This potent Mediatrix restores peace to those at war with Heaven; through her, pardon is accorded to the guilty, salvation is offered to those who are in despair. When Mary makes her voice heard, it is never on the side of war or vengeance ; *her* words are words of forgetfulness, pardon, peace.

Mary is the rainbow given to mankind as a pledge of reconciliation after the universal shipwreck of nature, lost by original sin; it is she who was figured by that mystic bow that St. John in the Apocalypse beheld around the throne of God—*Et iris erat in circuitu sedis.** Then if the Lord be justly angry with the world, if our crimes weigh down His arm upon us, let us cause this heavenly rainbow to shine before Him, this enduring pledge of pardon, Mary, whom he has set between Him and earth, to the end His mercy may always prevail over His justice. Ah! the Lord hath sworn and He will never repent—" I will set my bow in the clouds, a sign of peace, ... and in seeing it I will remember the everlasting covenant,"† which I have made with men.

Hard-hearted Christians who are indifferent to Mary, why are these consoling truths hidden from your eyes? Oh! avail yourselves of the day yet afforded you, prevent the vengeance of a God justly irritated, make use of the easy means offered you for concluding your peace with Heaven, through the mediation of Mary. O God! O Jesus! forget our crimes ; be mindful of Mary, through whom You have given Yourself to men ; hearken to this Mediatrix of peace, whose virtues, supplications, merits, are more powerful to honour You, than our crimes are capable of insult. And do you, our Mediatrix, exercise your functions ; Ark of the Covenant, appease Heaven! reassure earth.

* Apoc. iv.   † Gen. ix. 13.

Thirteenth Day.

O Mary, petition your only Son in favour of your adopted children; smooth the way that leads to this dear Son; obtain peace between the divine justice and my misery, that the Lord for your sake may forego His claims; supply what is wanting in my dispositions, that the just God may pronounce sentence of forgiveness; then shall all confess that you are the reconciliation of a sinful world with Heaven.

Practice.—We owe to Mary, as to God, a just proportion of exterior as well as interior worship. To salute her pictures and statues, bow when we pronounce her name, carry about us some token of devotion to this heavenly Queen, to join in the prayers publicly recited in the processions made in her honour, visit her sanctuaries, enter associations erected under her invocation, are all works most pleasing in her sight. Mary vouchsafes daily to recompense these by the most signal favours. Be then equally on your guard against the superstition which places all hope of salvation in these acts deprived of the lively faith that constitutes their merit, and against this proud reason that, under pretext of honouring God in spirit and in truth, rejects all exterior practice and demonstration, which are the natural evidence of interior conviction.

Aspiration.—O our Mediatrix! commend us to your Divine Son, reconcile us with Him.

Example.

Father Crasset assures us that he heard from a Colonel who had been an eye-witness, the following incident. At the close of a combat a wounded soldier was found on the field of battle, holding a rosary and scapular in his hand, and crying aloud for a confessor. This soldier had received in his forehead a ball, which naturally should have caused instantaneous death. Nevertheless he had sufficient strength to raise himself up and make his confession to the chaplain, with great sentiments of devotion and repentance, and after having received absolution he expired.

The same Colonel declared that he had witnessed a pistol shot fired almost at the breast of a soldier; they found that the ball had been stopped by a scapular which he wore, without grazing the skin, and that he took the ball and showed it to every one.*

* *Glories of Mary.*

FOURTEENTH DAY.

MARY IS OUR ADVOCATE.

"Let men confess that they have but one Advocate in Heaven, and that is you, O Mary!" (St. Augustine).

WE, all of us have an important suit to plead before the Judge of all justice; and this Judge is the person offended, this Judge is our God, our Creator, our Redeemer; it is against Himself, against His authority we have conspired. In His eyes, no one is just, no one is innocent, not even the infant of a day; the Angels were not found clean in His sight, and even our justices require expiation. A day will come when we shall be cited before His tribunal; no one can escape His judgment. He has observed all our ways He has examined our footsteps, nothing is concealed from Him. None can controvert His decrees; and if we venture to argue with Him, of a thousand accusations brought against us, we cannot refute a single one.

What shall we do, miserable that we are? Whither fly, where conceal ourselves? Who shall dare to speak for us, who become defender of a cause so desperate? Even she, the Mother of the Judge, the Mother of the culprit, Mary, who has constituted herself the Advocate of Christians. O sinners, whosoever you be, if the enormity, the horror of your crimes cause you to lose courage, if doubt entering into your soul, lead you also to say—" My sin is too great to be forgiven, my chastisement is due to God's justice;" in this excess of despondency, turn your eyes on Mary, and know that next to the title of Mother of God, there is none in which she glories more, than in that of Advocate of Sinners. The more desperate the cause you confide to her, the more worthy it is of her, the more pleasure God takes in suffering Himself to be disarmed, in order to prove the credit His Mother enjoys in Heaven.

Children of God, children of Mary, be not afraid to discover to this charitable Advocate all the wounds of your soul; to reveal to her the most secret motions of your heart, even those you dare not avow to yourself. The Heart of Mary is more sensible of your infirmity than you are; the more apparently irremediable it is, the more she is touched, the more eloquently she will plead in your favour.

St. Gertrude one day invoking the aid of Mary by these words of the *Salve Regina*—" Turn then, most gracious Advocate, thine eyes of mercy towards us," it appeared to her that this tender Mother was attracted to bend down towards her as if by powerful chains. And Mary made her understand that every time she is invoked as our Advocate, her maternal tenderness is so touched, that it is, as it were, impossible for her to resist such prayers. Our Lord Himself added, that whoever would invoke Mary, at least once a day in the same words—" Turn then, most gracious Advocate, thine eyes of mercy towards us," would undoubtedly derive succour at the hour of death.

Full of confidence in Mary, say then—" O Mother of Mercy, who, after your Divine Son, has had greater solicitude for poor mortals? Who consoles us like you in our afflictions? Who fights for sinners, who takes up arms in their defence like you,

Fourteenth Day.

O Mary?"* "Oh, how efficaciously, how lovingly this skilful Advocate pleads the cause of our salvation!"† "She never wearies of defending us."‡ So also St. Augustine, meditating on this zeal of Mary, cries out—"Let men acknowledge that they have in Heaven one only Advocate, and that is you, O Mother of Mercy!"

Dry your tears then, all you in tribulation; take courage, you whose cause is so desperate as to seem already lost; you who find none on earth to defend you, raise your eyes to Heaven; there you have an Advocate ever ready to speak in your favour; an Advocate so tender, so powerful, so ingenious in succouring you, that her Divine Son cannot condemn those whom she undertakes to vindicate. Then prostrate yourselves at her sacred feet, hold them in your embrace, and declare that you will not depart till she has spoken in your behalf, till she has blessed you.

Practice.—Make after each of your actions, or from hour to hour, "the examen of recollection." It consists in disavowing the faults that momentarily escape one, and placing oneself again in God's presence by renewing the desire to please Him. St. Ignatius, and many others after his example, attained to sanctity by assiduity to this practice of frequently turning to God. Alas! can we but feel alarmed at our want of circumspection in the affair of salvation, seeing the precautions, the means, employed by the Blessed Virgin herself and by the Saints to secure theirs?

Aspiration.—Turn then, most gracious Advocate, thine eyes of mercy towards us!

---

* St. Germanus.   † St. Bernard.
‡ St. Germanus.

Example.

In the year 1572 the learned Baronius was attacked by a severe illness, which reduced him to extremity. He had received the last Sacraments, and every moment was expected to be his last; but he had a Saint for his Superior and friend, St. Philip Neri, who had already recalled him from the gates of death. "Philip put himself in prayer to obtain anew the life of his cherished disciple. Presently Baronius fell into a sweet slumber, in which he beheld his Superior prostrate at the feet of the Saviour and of His holy Mother, imploring his restoration to health in these terms—'Lord, give me Baronius, restore him to me; I desire it, I wish it.' As Christ refused, he turned to His Mother; and Mary having interceded for him, he knew at once that he was heard. At the same moment Baronius awoke, with an internal conviction that he should not die of that illness. And, in effect, he recovered that very day, owing to his beloved Father his life and his doctrine, as he fails not to tell us in his *Annals*."*

So far the power of the Saints over Mary's Heart. But even sinners can count on its fidelity in the hour of need. A soldier having passed forty years in the forgetfulness of God and his religious duties, at last went in quest of a Priest and made his confession. The confessor, astonished, demanded whether he had not preserved some pious practice. "Do you know the 'Our Father'?" "I have forgotten it." "The 'Hail Mary'?" "I forget it also." "What prayer, then, do you say?" "I say none." "Impossible! search your memory

---

* Rohrbacher.

well. No one who has gone so far astray as you have, returns without having retained some religious custom." "I do not remember having done more than repeat occasionally these words, which I had heard sung in childhood—

> In thee, O Mary, I confide,
> Be thou my helper and my guide;
> My soul from all its foes defend,
> O Virgin, keep me to the end.
> And when at last the hour is come
> Which shall decide my eternal doom,
> Obtain that I may tranquilly
> Breathe forth my soul to God and thee.

I hoped, too, to be converted some day, and through our Blessed Lady's intercession to obtain the grace of a happy death."

FIFTEENTH DAY.

MARY'S POWER.

"O Mary, you will, and all things are accomplished" (St. Bernard).

TO God alone be honour and glory! He alone is great; He alone can do all things. Nevertheless, all power has been given to Mary in Heaven and on earth. Wherefore? Because she is the Mother of the Almighty, Who has placed in her hands the fulness of His authority. Jesus Christ Himself deigned to be subject to her upon earth, in quality of Son. "For if it may be said of other virgins, that 'they follow the Lamb whithersoever He goeth,' it may be said of Mary that the Lamb followed her on earth everywhere she went, according to these words of St. Luke—'He was subject to them.'"* In Heaven she no longer commands her Divine Son, yet he has preserved to her all her prerogatives. Jesus is all-powerful by nature, Mary by grace; it is for us, for our interests, she employs this unlimited authority. A single word of Mary's here was omnipotent with Jesus. The hour of this Divine Master was not yet come: Mary knew it; yet, touched with compassion for that privileged couple whose union she blessed by her presence, she said to Him, "They have no wine." Then, certain of being heard, notwithstanding the mysterious response that she received, she bade the servants to do all that He should tell them, and the miracle was accomplished. Let us then go, we also, to

* Richard of St. Laurence.

Mary; she will obtain a revocation of the sentence passed in Heaven against our sinful souls. If she was so touched at the confusion of her hosts, and rewarded with such liberality the invitation she had received, what will she not do for those devoted to her, who press her to abide in their souls, not temporally or occasionally, but all the days of their pilgrimage? Oh! in what lively colours will she paint their spiritual necessities to her Divine Son, saying once more—" They have no wine!" The wine of charity, of piety, fails them, pour it into their hearts; their steps are tottering, strengthen them; their arms fall through lassitude, uphold them; their heart wavers, give them a share of your immutability; they can do nothing of themselves, give them that ardent faith which renders all things possible.

Yes, what God effects by His will, Mary obtains by prayer: she is (as a holy Father says) that all-powerful suppliant who may not be refused. Jesus could not be deaf to the prayers of His Mother, and has imposed upon Himself a law, to grant all her requests. It is related in the *Revelations of St. Bridget*, that she heard our Lord thus address His Mother—" Ask, O Mother, whatever your wish; never shall your petitions be without effect. . . . Since you denied Me nothing while I was on earth, I will refuse you nothing in Heaven." St. Gertrude beheld the Queen of Heaven bearing in her hand a scroll, on which were inscribed those words so frequently addressed to her by the Church: " May the Virgin intercede for us "—*Ipsa intercedat pro peccatis nostris*. And she heard our Lord say to Mary—" In virtue of My omnipotence, O My revered Mother, I have delegated to you the faculty of remitting, as it shall please you, the sins of all who devoutly implore your compassionate succour."*

O Mary! you have then but to will, and all things are accomplished—*Velis tu, et omnia fient.*† You command, and nothing resists you. Bid, then, my soul come forth from the state of sin, of languor, of tepidity, in which it groans, and happiness and peace shall once more be its portion; command my enemies to take flight, and they shall be humbled, they shall be confounded.

Practice.—Mary, without doubt, desires and has the power to assist us; but how many there are who, by their coldness of heart and irresolution of will, frustrate this tender Mother's solicitude for their salvation! Ask, then, through Mary this constant, efficacious, ardent *will*, which entirely absorbs the soul in the pursuit of the sovereign good, which is God; that *iron will* which breaks, overthrows, tramples under foot every obstacle; in a word, this *goodwill* to which the Angels promised, on the part of God, a peace which is the foretaste of the enjoyment of Heaven.

Aspiration.—Thy will be done on earth in my irresolute heart, O Jesus, as it was unceasingly accomplished in the Heart of Mary!

Example.

A zealous Missionary, famed for his winning and persuasive eloquence, had preached the Devotion of the Living Rosary at Perigneux without success. The Bishop, a Prelate highly commendable for his piety and truly episcopal virtues, had deemed it his duty to beg he would desist from urging it any

---

* Bk. iv., ch. liii.   † St. Bernard.

farther, persuaded that this practice could not yet be established there. The time appointed by God had not yet arrived for this city. When the holy person destined by the Almighty to revive St. Dominic's Devotion of the Rosary presented herself at Perigneux, she met opposition in all quarters. Nobody would introduce her to his lordship; people refused to speak in her favour to the Vicar General, and she spent her first day in knocking to no purpose at all the doors. At length, as evening drew near, she meets a Priest and inquires if he can introduce her to the Vicar General. "I am he," replied the clergyman. "I am M. P——," she said; "and wish very much to have a conversation with the Bishop." "Certainly, it will afford him great pleasure to see you." He accordingly escorted her to the episcopal residence. The Prelate, on seeing her enter, exclaimed—"Welcome, Miss P——. I was impatiently expecting you, as I knew you were to pass through Perigneux. You are probably aware that I deemed it prudent some months since to defer the establishment of the Rosary here; but now I have just written to all the Parish Priests of the diocese to propagate it. To this I have been induced by the following occurrence. Visiting the prisons one day in company with the Vicar here, for the purpose of administering some consolation to the inmates, after I had made the round of the dungeons, the gaoler told me there was only one more, in which was confined an unfortunate criminal who was to be executed that very day; but that it would be risking my life to enter, he was so furious; no one dared even to bring him food. 'Only the greater reason I should go to his assistance; open the door, I command you,'

I said. The door opened, and revealed to us the wretched man, who in his despair had climbed, no one could say how, up into the window, which was more than eight feet high, and was trying to dash out his brains against the iron bars. When he perceived us, his fury redoubled; he cast himself precipitately down, expecting to crush us in his fall, at the same time uttering reproaches and blasphemies. We had just time to retire hastily and lock the door. I then sent word to all the Religious Communities in the town that, ceasing all occupations, they should recite the Rosary for this unfortunate man. The Vicar and I recited it likewise. The prayer terminated, 'Come,' said I, 'let us return to the prison: our man is converted.' They endeavoured to dissuade me. The gaoler refused to open the door, on the plea that he would be accountable should an accident occur. However, I ordered him to obey, adding that I took on myself all the consequences. We entered at last, and what did we behold? O prodigy of grace! the wolf has become a lamb —he was on his knees in prayer. Seeing us, he cast himself at our feet, bathed in tears. 'Ah! my lord,' he said, 'forgive my conduct, grant me your blessing. Our Lord deigned to pardon the thief on the Cross; He is not less powerful now that He is in Heaven. Yes, I hope He will grant me remission of all my sins.' He then asked to confess. The Vicar spends two hours with him; the sobs of the culprit accompanied the avowal of his crimes. He received absolution with the deepest sentiments of contrition and gratification. The officers of justice arriving shortly after, proceeded to read his sentence. 'Stay, gentlemen,' interrupted he, 'here begins my Way of the Cross;

this is my first Station.' Then, placing himself on his knees, in this humble posture he listened to his death-warrant; after which he said aloud, 'My God, I accept death with all my heart, in atonement for my crimes.' Then, accompanied by the Vicar, who would not leave him, he followed the officers. At the foot of the prison stairs he prostrated himself once more, and prayed for a short time; and thus he continued stopping from time to time in the streets and squares of the city. Arriving before a church, he requested the procession to halt. Then, with his face bowed down to the ground, he cried out—'My God, I am not worthy to enter Your holy temple, but I desire to make reparation at the door for all the insults and sacrileges of which I have been guilty.' He did this in so feeling a manner, that the spectators were affected to tears. He arose and walked to the place of execution, where he again prayed for a moment. Then the Vicar, raising his voice, said to the crowd surrounding the scaffold—'Let us say a *Pater* and *Ave* for the criminal.' The entire assembly fell on their knees; emotion, joy, grief, admiration, choked their utterance—naught but sobs were to be heard. With the termination of the prayer, the penitential course of the unfortunate culprit had also ended." "Judge if, after this," said his lordship to Miss P——, "I ought not to propagate the Devotion of the Rosary."

SIXTEENTH DAY.

ALL GOOD THINGS COME TO US THROUGH MARY.

Omnia per Mariam.

WHATEVER good we possess, it is to the Blood, sufferings, and tears of Jesus our Redeemer we are indebted. But to whom, after God, are we indebted for Jesus Himself, if not to His Mother, to Mary? And giving us this immense good, could she fail to give us every other good with Him? "How hath He not also with Him given us all things?"* Or who can wonder that Jesus, having delivered Himself over to Mary, should have remitted to her all the spiritual riches consequent upon this first gift? Rejoice then, ye children of this tender Mother, and say boldly— "All good things came to me together with Mary."† Yes, he who has found this source of graces, has found all virtues, since there is nothing that Mary's intercession cannot obtain for him; it is she who says—"With me are riches and glory . . . that I may enrich them that love me."‡ All the goods, all the graces, all the helps men have received or shall receive from God to the end of time, have been or shall be derived from the intercession, through the interposition, of Mary. It is from the plenitude of gifts showered upon her by her Divine Son, that we have become enriched. "Of His fulness we all have received."§ Accordingly, St. Bonaventure counsels us never to turn aside our

---

* Rom. viii. 32.   † Wisdom.   ‡ Prov. viii.
§ St. John i. 16.

eyes from Mary, that thus we may secure to ourselves a share in the blessings that are continually dispensed at her hands.

St. Cajetan affirms — "That no matter how earnestly we may petition for grace, it is only through the intercession of Mary we shall obtain it;" and St. Antoninus adds — "To ask otherwise than through her, is to attempt to fly without wings." "I have appointed thee over the whole land of Egypt," Pharaoh said to Joseph; and to all who had recourse to him, he replied — "Go to Joseph."* When we ask any favour from God, He refers us to Mary, so that Christians may say to Mary with far greater reason than the Egyptians said to Joseph — "Our salvation is in thy hands."

O Mary, through whom all good has come to us, Virgin full of grace, may all Christians, as St. Bernard so beautifully expresses himself, "honour you with their whole heart, cling to you with the utmost tenacity." May they be sensible that all share in your favours, that you forsake none, despise none, but invite all to avail themselves of your unbounded power!

Invoke her, then, all who would avoid perishing, who aspire to a life of immortality. Just and fervent souls, invoke Mary that she may sustain you in the steep and narrow path of rectitude, that ascending from virtue to virtue, you may reach the summit of the holy mountain where God crowns His elect. Imperfect and tepid souls, who carry the yoke of the Lord so slothfully, invoke Mary that she may hasten to reanimate your sluggishness, before God reject you entirely out of His mouth, and your wayward heart, to borrow a Scripture expression,

---

* Gen. xli. 45.

return to its vomit. And you, sinners, who plunged in an abyss of the most shameful disorders, feel the horror of your condition, but despair of extricating yourself, who believe not the possibility of breaking chains so heavy, of overcoming habits so inveterate, have recourse to Mary, with her aid everything is possible to you.*

Practice.—Whatever you ask, ask it through Mary; present through her hands all your prayers and good works to God. Yield her this homage of the heart, of which she is so jealous, accustoming yourself to act as if she were present—under her direction; begging her blessing at the commencement of your principal actions with the same confidence as if you beheld her face to face.

Aspiration.—You shall not die for ever, my soul! you shall live again to grace, in order to relate the marvels of Mary's power—*Non moriar sed vivam!*

Example.

In the fifteenth century, when the exertions of Blessed Alain de la Roche caused the almost forgotten Devotion of the Rosary to revive, there dwelt in the south of France a noble lady who governed her house with a holy regularity, and who was one of the first to join the confraternity on its re-establishment. She had an only son, named Bernard, an amiable child, ennobled no less by his disposition than by his birth, and above all distinguished by an angelic innocence of life. His mother sent him to a neighbouring school for the prosecution of his studies, whence he returned every evening. It does not appear that Bernard

* M'Carthy.

wanted abilities, he even made remarkable progress, but the composition of French and Latin verses, one of the most frequent duties of his school, presented insurmountable difficulties to him. The poor youth passed many a weary hour in fruitless attempts. His want of success had rendered him the laughing-stock of his companions, and not unfrequently drew down upon him the punishment of his masters. Returning home one evening after a day more than usually disastrous, he gave way to most despondent thoughts. His mother questioned him affectionately; Bernard gave no reply. "You do not speak, my child. You were never accustomed to hide your griefs from your mother; is it that you have committed some grave fault that you fear to acknowledge?" "No mother," he replied, "it is only that people call me imbecile, stupid, and their judgment is correct; but although my feelings are deeply wounded, it is no grave fault, but simply, I am not a poet." "What, is this all that distresses you? Why envy a gift which brings so little happiness, and sometimes weakens divine grace in the soul? Aspire to higher favours; piety of heart, and an ardent faith, are acquisitions worthier your ambition." "My mother, you know not what is thought of me; and I shall remain the scorn of my schoolfellows, even as I already am, so long as I am incapable of making verses; and make them I never shall," he added sadly. "Bernard," rejoined his mother, "I do not flatter myself I can help you in making verses, but it may be I shall succeed in raising your courage. Master Alain de la Roche lately told us of a student to whom books were as wearisome as poetry can be to you; yet he not only found means to understand them, but even to write some himself, and he died one of the most celebrated doctors of the University." "How did he accomplish this?" asked Bernard. "By very simple means," rejoined his mother; "he besought the aid of the Blessed Virgin, reciting daily the Rosary in her honour. What prevents you from doing the same? Master Alain gave you a beads, of which you do not make much use; recite it before the altar of the Mother of God every day before going to class; say the prayers as he has taught you, and remember that no one ever yet prayed to Mary and did not obtain her assistance." Bernard followed his mother's advice; and not content to say a part of the Rosary, he daily recited the Fifteen Mysteries on his knees before the statue of the Blessed Virgin. A complete metamorphosis was in a short time effected in his mind. Not only all difficulty disappeared, but Bernard's compositions displayed a depth of thought and singular elegance of imagery, which soon became perceptible to all; and those who had formerly surpassed him were left speedily behind. How could it have been otherwise? His soul delighted to drink at the genuine sources of moral beauty, and by daily meditation on those Joyful, Sorrowful, and Glorious Mysteries, he penetrated the ineffable secrets of that Life and Passion, the copious well-spring of all that is elevated, tender, and true in sentiment. The sacred names which were ever on his lips, and the presence of Mary which everywhere overshadowed him, were for him an unfailing though invisible assistance. Each day he felt the maternal eyes of compassion, which he so often invoked, beaming sweetly on him. This familiar intercourse warmed his understanding with the flames of divine love; and whilst others extolled their favourite poets, Mary was his theme—

he acknowledged himself indebted to her for all his inspirations.

The masters marvelled at the transformation of their pupil: they pretended to account for it by subtle reasonings on the development of intellect; the pupils wondered no less, and ere long addressed themselves to Bernard, beseeching him to help them in their compositions. As to this last, if people praised him, or if they asked whence he derived his thoughts and poetical images, he declared with admirable ingenuousness, that by reciting the Rosary every one could do as much. This unfailing reply was soon caught up by his companions, who bestowed on him the name of "Scholar of the Rosary."

What was to become of this boy? The most exalted destiny was predicted for him. Nevertheless, conjecture and previsions were alike at fault, and for the pupil of Mary was reserved a fortune superior to those of earth. The world was not worthy of him. Returning home one day, Bernard complained to his mother of a great pain in his eyes; on the morrow inflammation became general, and spread so rapidly that he could not bear the light, and he suffered the most violent pains. Bernard, however, despite his ailment and increasing weakness, failed not to recite his entire Rosary. He consoled his mother when she lamented his threatened blindness, by assuring her that his Devotion by its own nature afforded him ample distraction, and that one charming feature in it was that it required neither sight, nor even the aid of books to nourish it, the mere touch of his beloved beads, which he always wore round his neck, sufficing to testify to Mary the sentiments of his heart. Blindness, alas! was not the only trial the poor mother had to fear, it now became evident that the malady had reached that fatal point to which no human remedy can bring alleviation. Bernard must go to contemplate the glory, and sing with the Angels the praises of her whom he had so fondly loved on earth. If the thought of the sacrifice about to be required from her cost the pious mother many a pang, this cross was not without its consolation also; she knew the admirable innocence of her Bernard, and felt that she was confiding the dear child to the arms of a Mother whose tenderness exceeded her own. Nor was Mary slow in justifying this trust. Before the administration of the last rites of the Church to the sufferer, his mother, in anticipation of the Priest's arrival, ordered the chamber to be lighted up, although the physicians had prescribed total darkness. "What need is there of light here?" asked Bernard. "It is for the Priest, my child," answered the mother; "you will try and bear it for a few minutes." "But there is light already; the room is full of it," rejoined he; "to me it has never been dark. I am astonished you do not perceive it." "What light," asked the Priest, who had now entered. "Your mother and I are beside you, but to our eyes the chamber is in complete darkness." "The light proceeds from our Lady," replied Bernard; "she is here beside me, her glory shines on and enlightens me. Since I fell sick, I have never been in the dark." A holy fear filled the Priest, and he involuntarily bowed respectfully in the direction pointed out by the patient, at the same time asking him—"And does not this light hurt your eyes; you, who cannot tolerate daylight?" "This light is joy," answered Bernard, in tones of rapture; "it is for me joy and glory. All pain is now over." Thus died, a few moments after, this child of benediction. Those he left behind him, experienced a heartfelt assurance that "Mary's scholar" enjoyed in its plenitude this glory, the reflection of which had lighted up his bed of death.

SEVENTEENTH DAY.

MARY SUCCOURS HER SERVANTS IN THEIR LAST MOMENTS.

"Though I walk in the midst of the shadow of death, I will not fear," O Mary, *"for thou art with me"* (Psalm xxii. 4).

THERE are decisive moments in the life of the soul, attractive and victorious graces, whose influence rules, so to say, her entire existence; every instant brings us nearer to the immortal throne in Heaven, or to the bottomless pit of hell. Nevertheless, it is yet true to say that our eternity is attached and as it were suspended more definitely still on that one moment which will be our last. *Ab uno momento pendet æternitas.* If the enemy of souls, maddened at the prospect of losing his prey, redoubles his stratagems and efforts to rob Christ of His victory, it is also at this moment of death that Mary displays the manifold resources of her love and power in behalf of her servants. Unlike earthly friends, who desert those dearest to them when they see them in affliction, or poverty, it is in such circumstances she more munificently rewards their past confidence and love towards her. Not content to succour her servants during life, she displays still greater eagerness to soothe their final hour; for, as she assured St. Bridget, "She dever fails to assist, whether visibly or invisibly, at the death-bed of such as have served her faithfully during life. And who could enumerate the friends for whom she has transformed a day so formidable into the fairest and happiest of existence; and who, consoled and sustained by this divine Mother, have cried out with their dying breath—"Ah! I did not think it was so sweet to die."* Faithful children of Mary, you, whose earthly career, nay, whose very devotion to her, may have been fraught with trials and desolation, expect your Mother, expect her even to the end; you have sown in tears, you shall reap at that last hour in transports of joy; it is *then* that Mary has resolved to make amends for all the consolation denied during life.

A zealous servant of Mary being assisted at death by Father Binetti, said, when about to breathe his last sigh—"O Father, did you but know the comfort I feel for having been devout to the Blessed Virgin. I cannot express the rapture I experience at this moment." Father Manuel Padial lying on his death-bed, Mary appeared to him, and addressed him in these consoling words—"The hour is come at last when the Angels, rejoicing with thee, will say, 'O happy labours! O mortifications amply rewarded!'" Another, being violently tempted against faith, at once recommended himself to Mary, and was heard to cry out—"O Mary, I thank you for coming to my assistance." St. John of God, on his death-bed awaited a visit from Mary. Not seeing her appear, he complained to Mary herself with sorrow. The opportune time arrived. She did not fail to come, and making him some gentle reproaches on his want of confidence, she uttered these tender words, which may well rouse the faith of all Mary's servants—"John, I am not the one to desert my servants at their last hour."

Let us then recite, with renewed feelings of faith

* Suarez.

and confidence, that prayer which the Church puts so frequently on our lips—" Holy Mary, Mother of God, pray for us sinners now and at the hour of our death." Pray for us at that hour, through which all must pass, at that hour which will decide our eternity, and in which you are accustomed to signalize your mercy in favour of your devoted children. Oh, then, at this dread hour, when I shall walk in the shadow of death, be you my guide, forsake me not ; for what evil can I fear, if you be with me? " I will fear no evils, for thou art with me."* Frustrate the hopes of my enemies, let me expire in your arms, and from the arms of my Mother be borne into the Heart of my Jesus, in Which, and through Which, O Mary, I will sing thy mercies eternally—*Misericordias Mariæ cantabo in æternum.*

Oh, yes! the chains that attach us to Mary are salutary bands ; they shall be our rest at the last day. " Her bands are a healthful binding ; in the latter end thou shalt find rest in her."† St. Camillus de Lellis, whose especial vocation it was to assist the agonizing, was accustomed to say to his Religious—" Remind the dying frequently to invoke the names of Jesus and Mary." He experienced the efficacy of this pious practice himself. His biographer relates that in his last moments he pronounced the names of Jesus and Mary in accents so tender that all present felt their hearts moved and inflamed ; and with his eyes fixed on their image, his arms extended in the form of a cross, he breathed forth his soul, with a countenance on which the joys of Paradise were already painted. This short prayer, "Jesus, Mary," to which

* Psalm xxii. 4. † Wisdom vi.

the Church has attached a Plenary Indulgence, in favour of her children at the hour of death, "is easy to retain, pleasant to dwell upon, and all powerful against the enemy," who is then busy laying his last snares against us.

O Mary! will I say to you with St. Bonaventure, for the glory of your name, when my soul shall have departed this life, hasten to meet and welcome it. Comfort it with the view of your benign countenance, be its ladder, its path to Heaven. Obtain pardon for it, procure a place for it in the kingdom of eternal light. "Ah, may the last movement of my lips be to pronounce your sweet name, O Mother of God!"* "O sweet death, happy death, which is protected by this saving name, for it is only those whom God intends to save, to whom He gives the power to invoke it."† O Mary! I will repeat your admirable name so often during life, that familiarity will place it on my lips even when consciousness shall have abandoned me; bearing this olive branch in my mouth, when I present myself before your Divine Son, I cannot but be favourably received.

Practice. — This special grace of protection towards her dying servants, Mary has in some sort merited by submitting to death herself, after her Divine Son's example, and in exercising at this supreme moment the most heroic acts of humility and love. One of the surest means of meriting her assistance at the dread instant, is to treasure up the memory of that holy death, pondering thereon, and beseeching her to render our last end like to hers. The Church commemorates the decease of the Blessed Virgin on the 12th of

---

* St. Germanus.   † St. Ligouri.

August, three days before the Feast of her glorious Assumption.

Aspiration.—May my soul die the death of the just,* the death of your devoted servant, O Mary!

Example.

There dwelt at Reisburg, a Canon Regular named Arnaud, who was extremely devout to the Blessed Virgin. This Canon, feeling the approach of his last hour, received the last Sacraments, and summoning his Religious, besought them not to abandon him on this momentous occasion. The request would seem to proceed from a secret presentiment of what was to follow, for hardly had it been made, than in their presence a most terrible combat began. Arnaud trembled in all his members, a cold perspiration bathed his face, he cast terrified glances towards some object invisible to all eyes save his own. "Do you not see," he said, in an altered tone, "the devils who surround me? they wish to carry me off to hell. My brethren, invoke Mary's aid for me; it is in her I put my trust." Forthwith the Religious began the Litany of the Blessed Virgin, and when they came to the words—"Holy Mary, pray for him," the dying man interrupted them, saying—"Repeat the name of Mary, for I am now before the tribunal of God." Then, after a short pause, he resumed, as if in answer to his accuser—"Yes, I did all that, but I have done penance for it." Then, addressing the Holy Virgin, he cried out—"O Mary, I shall conquer my enemies, if you but come to my assistance." The night passed in these frightful assaults,

* Numb. xxiii. 10.

to which he ceased not to oppose his crucifix and the holy name of Mary; but with the day, calm returned, and Arnaud, with a serene countenance, joyfully announced that Mary, his refuge, had obtained his eternal salvation. Then turning towards the Blessed Virgin, who invited him to follow her, he said—"I come, my Mistress, I come," and making an effort to rise, he expired. His soul, we may hope, following Mary, in default of his body, into the kingdom of eternal glory.*

* Auriemna, quoted by St. Ligouri.

EIGHTEENTH DAY.

MARY SUCCOURS HER SERVANTS IN PURGATORY.

"*I have walked on the waves of the sea*" (Ecclus. xxiv. 8).

THERE is an abode of expiatory suffering where the souls of the just lament far away from God, Whom they were only allowed to contemplate for a moment on their departure from this world, but to render the delay of their happiness still more insupportable.

What are the pains endured in this sorrowful region of Purgatory? The same as those of hell, if we except the damnation. The soul in Purgatory loves God, but feels that her faults disqualify her for consummate union with Him in Heaven; she rushes towards Him with irresistible impetuosity, then withdraws herself, through a just sentiment of her own unworthiness with a heart-rending, of which the bitterest griefs, separations, most overwhelming losses of this life, can furnish no idea. This is her first and most grievous torture—the pain of *loss*, the privation of God, which makes her in some measure to esteem as nought the pains of *sense*, though these surpass the most intolerable in this world. Because if she suffers, she is willing to suffer, and thus satisfy God's justice, Whose will in all things she loves and adores.

What is the matter of these incomparable torments? Faults which we regard as trivial, which pass unperceived in our superficial examens, duties omitted, negligence in the fulfilment of our obligations, sins confessed but not expiated, virtues and good works in which self-love had a share—

sins slight only in our own eyes. For if a cup of cold water given in the name of Jesus Christ shall not remain unrewarded, neither shall the idle word be suffered to rest unatoned for. Even, to privileged souls, a momentary cooling in the love of God, Who has displayed Himself more clearly to them, merits expiation. In a word, wood, branches, straw, shall be tried in the fire, only gold shall be proof against it.

Wholly absorbed in the fleeting interests of this life, accustomed as we are to form our estimate of the things of eternity according to the low standard of those of time, we have not a sufficiently elevated idea of the purity of soul God requires in order to our union with Him, of the punishment our culpable omissions, our base ingratitude, merit. We think too lightly of Purgatory, and are heedless in shunning the faults there expiated; we do not sufficiently compassionate the souls detained there, nor are we zealous enough in affording them relief.

But these poor souls have one Advocate that never fails them, Mary, who, having loved her servants who were in the world, loves them to the end, after the example of her Divine Son. Not content with assisting at their last struggle, and frustrating the hopes of the enemy in this decisive battle, she, moreover, with the Angels, presents their souls at the tribunal of divine justice, dispelling their fears by her sweet presence, and it is she who succours and relieves them in Purgatory. "The more pitiable the condition of these souls, who are incapable of assisting themselves, the more zealous is Mary in love and solicitude towards them." St. Bernardine of Sienna assures us that the Queen of Heaven exercises a certain sway over that prison in which divine justice purifies the spouses of Jesus Christ. He applies these words of Ecclesiasticus to the Blessed Virgin —"I have walked on the waves of the sea," comparing the pains of Purgatory to waves generally, because they are transient, and likening them to the "waves of the *sea*," as they have its bitterness. Now Mary descends into these gloomy depths, and walks on these most bitter waves to console her children and alleviate their sufferings. "See how it imports us to serve this great lady faithfully," says Novarinus, "seeing that she forgets not her clients when they are in flames; and though all the souls in Purgatory experience the aid of Mary, yet she assists in a special manner those among them who had been more devout to her during life."

Our Lady said to St. Bridget—"I am the Mother of all the souls in Purgatory, inasmuch as not an hour passes but their sufferings are mitigated through my intercession. The sole name of Mary, when it echoes through this abode of pain, becomes a relief similar to that given to a sick person by the soothing words of consolation." The prayers of the Blessed Virgin for the suffering souls are as a dew descending on these flames and tempering their intolerable ardour.

To relieve her clients is but little; Mary even breaks their chains. We learn from a pious tradition, and Gerson has left it in writing, that, on the day of her glorious Assumption, "Purgatory was left empty." Novarinus confirms it. "Grave authors relate," he says, "that the Blessed Virgin, at her death, solicited and obtained of her Son the favour of leading in her train all the souls detained in that place of expiation." From that time "she has enjoyed the privilege of liberating her faithful servants from the pains of Purgatory," and through her merits "the sufferings of these souls are not alone alleviated, but are even abridged."

St. Peter Damian tells us that a certain Marosia appearing after death, to a person of her acquaintance, told her that, on the Feast of the Assumption, she had been released from Purgatory with such a number of other souls as exceeded the population of Rome. St. Denis the Carthusian affirms that "Mary also descends into Purgatory on the solemn Feasts of the Nativity and Resurrection of Christ, attended by legions of Angels, and delivers a vast number of souls;" a deed of charity which happens on all her own Festivals, according to Novarinus.

Why not hope for the same favours and graces for ourselves, if we cherish a true devotion towards this Holy Mother? Who knows but she will do yet more for us, if she will not obtain that our souls may be so completely purified on earth that we may be permitted to enjoy the beatific vision without passing through Purgatory? This is what she did for Blessed Godfrey. "Go," said Mary to Brother Abondas, "and tell Brother Godfrey to advance in virtue; he shall then belong to my Son and me, and when his soul shall be separated from his body I will not suffer it to fall into Purgatory, but will receive it and myself present it to my Son."

Practice.—If we desire to relieve the souls in Purgatory, let us endeavour to interest the Blessed Virgin in their favour by our prayers, above all by applying to them the many Indulgences which can be gained by the recital of the beads, by fervent

* St. Ligouri.

Communions, &c. Mary is greatly pleased with those who form the intention to relieve in particular those souls that, during life, were remarkable for a more ardent devotion to this divine Mother. Whatever you shall have done to the least of her servants, that will she reckon as done to herself.

Aspiration.—O Mary! what could I do worthy of you? Nevertheless, I have a firm trust that you will be mindful of me at the last day.

Example.

We read in the Life of Sister Catherine of St. Augustine that a woman named Mary lived in her vicinity, who from early youth had led a career of vice. Age brought no amendment, so that her fellow-citizens, tired of her excesses, determined to banish her to a grotto situated on the confines of their country. Here, her body wasted by a loathsome disease, which caused the flesh to drop off in pieces, she died in a short time, without Sacraments and deprived of all human aid. Such a death was deemed undeserving the honours of sepulture, consequently she was not interred in consecrated ground. Sister Catherine, who had the pious custom of specially recommending to God the souls of such of her acquaintance as passed out of this life, thought not of the old sinner, believing her damned, according to the general opinion. Four years had already elapsed since the death of this woman, when the servant of God, being in prayer one day, a soul from Purgatory appeared to her and said—"Sister Catherine, how unfortunate I am! You pray for all that die; my poor soul is the only one on whom you have no compassion." "And who are you?" asked the servant of God. "I am," replied the soul, "that poor Mary who died in the grotto." "What! you saved!" exclaimed Catherine, in amazement. "Yes, I am, through the commiseration of the Blessed Virgin," she answered. "In my last moments, abandoned by all, and seeing myself defiled with such multiplied crimes, I addressed myself to the Mother of God, and said to her from the bottom of my heart— 'O you, who art the refuge of the forsaken, have pity on me, who am abandoned by the whole world. You are my only hope; come to my assistance.' I did not pray in vain. Through her intercession I obtained grace to make an act of perfect contrition, and thus escaped hell. Our Lady, moreover, has procured the abridgment of my pains, divine justice making me suffer in intensity what otherwise I must have suffered in duration. A few Masses are all that is now required to deliver me from Purgatory; get them offered for me, and I promise that, once admitted into Heaven, I will not cease to supplicate God and His holy Mother for you." Sister Catherine caused the Masses to be celebrated, and some days after she appeared to her anew, more brilliant than the sun, and, after many expressions of gratitude, said to her—"Heaven is at last open to me; I go there to sing the divine mercies, and be assured you shall not be forgotten."

NINETEENTH DAY.

MARY IS THE GATE OF HEAVEN.

"By me Kings reign" (Prov. viii. 15).

HEAVEN, that house of our eternity, that native land from which we are all expatriated, that place of rest in which this world, with its turmoils, shall be obliterated from our remembrance, that abode of delights, where God, manifesting himself in all His glory, shall fill the immense capacity of our hearts. Heaven! alas! how rarely we reflect on, how little we desire it! And yet, what do we expect—what seek we here below? If a solitary ray of that light that shines in the great day of eternity would beam upon us, how would we be consumed with longings for its blissful enjoyment! If we do not feel it, if we do not comprehend it, at least we believe that Heaven is the term of our course, the only worthy object of our ambition. But who, O Lord, shall reach this magnificent abode? Who shall dwell in your tabernacles—who rest for ever among your Elect and Saints in this blissful region, where death shall no more exert its sway, where lamentation and groaning shall be heard no more, where You will deign to wipe away with Your own hands the traces of all tears shed on earth? *Domine, quis habitabit in tabernaculo tuo aut quis requiescet in monte sancto tuo?** To this St. Bonaventure replies—"He who will follow in the footsteps of Mary, and will not leave her till she gives him her

* Psalm xli. 4.

blessing, because if she desire our salvation it is assured." In effect she herself tells us—"It is by me Kings reign in this kingdom, which counts as many monarchs as citizens; by me they conquer their passions, and secure that eternal dominion wherein they shall for ever enjoy the fruits of their victory. *Per me reges regnant;* * *Quot cives tot reges.*"† For, according to the expression of Richard of St. Laurence, Mary is the mistress of Paradise; she commands there, introduces there whom she pleases. And is it not just that she should rule there, should there exercise authority, since she is the Mother of the Lord of Heaven? "You, then, who desire to enter this mansion of bliss, Mary is the gate which is never closed, because he who serves Mary, for whom she intercedes, is as sure of Heaven as if in actual possession of it."‡ "Yes, O Mary, all who confide in your protection shall see the gates of Heaven opened to admit them.§ So that, according to St. Ephrem, devotion to the Blessed Virgin may be called the key of Paradise. Let us, therefore, without ceasing say to her—"Open to us, O holy Virgin, open Heaven to us, of which you have the keys!— *Aperi nobis, O Virgo! cœlum cujus claves habes.*"‖

Again, the Church styles Mary the "Star of the Sea"—*Stella maris*, because, as mariners steer towards port by the inspection of the stars, so, by keeping their eyes fixed on Mary, Christians reach the kingdom of glory. St. Mary Magdalen de Pazzi saw a bark sailing on the sea of this life, which served as a refuge for all the clients of Mary, and

---

* Prov. viii. 15.   † St. Augustine.   ‡ Guerric.
§ St. Bonaventure.   ‖ St. Ambrose.

the Queen of Heaven, acting as pilot, steered them without accident into port. St. Peter Damian styles the Blessed Virgin the "Ladder of Heaven;" for as it was through her God came down from Heaven, so through her men might merit to ascend from earth to Heaven. We read in the Franciscan chronicles that Brother Leo had the following vision—"He beheld two ladders; one red, at the summit of which stood Jesus Christ, the other white, at the top of which was His holy Mother. Many tried to ascend the first ladder, but after mounting a few steps they fell to the ground. They returned to the charge, with no better success; not one reached the summit. Whereupon a voice cried out to them to turn to the white ladder, and having done so they scaled it in safety, for the Blessed Virgin held out her hand to assist them."

But do we desire a still further guarantee of the efficacy of this Devotion to the Mother of God in order to obtain Paradise? We find it in the words of Mary herself. Addressing her faithful clients, and in particular those who strive to propagate devotion to her, she says—"They that work by me shall not sin. They that explain me shall have life everlasting."* The Lord Himself unites with the Queen of Heaven, when He says, in the Apocalypse—"He that shall overcome, I will write upon him the name of my God, and the name of the city of my God."† Now that city of God is none other than the most pure Virgin Mary. "Glorious things are said of thee, O city of God."‡

* Ecclus. xxiv. 30, 31.   † Apoc. iii. 12.
‡ Psalm lxxxvi. 3.

Practice. — "He that lives without rule lives without reason," said one of the ancients; "He that lives according to rule lives according to God," adds St. Gregory of Nyssa. Lay down a plan of life for yourself, then, which will leave none of your actions to caprice and the indecision of the moment. By this means you shall avoid idleness, with its countless train of faults, and shall amass for yourself a treasure of merits for Heaven. If subject to a rule observe it faithfully; bless God for furnishing you so excellent means of perfection, and remember that the holiness of the Saints was the fruit of their fidelity to the rule they had embraced.

Aspiration.—Open to us, O open to us, holy Virgin, the Heart of Jesus—that Heaven of which you hold the keys—*Aperi nobis, O Virgo! cœlum cujus claves habes.**

Example.

The Blessed Virgin has invariably watched over her servants at that decisive period when they must enter the world and choose a state of life, because on this choice, on this moment, depends nearly always the after career and even the eternal welfare. Tancred, favourite of the Emperor Frederic II., is a convincing proof of this. This young nobleman, calling to mind the danger to which his salvation would be exposed in the world, had recourse to Mary, and implored her, by the credit she enjoys with God, to make known to him in what state he can more readily secure his salvation. He redoubled his prayers, made them with greater fervour,

* St. Ambrose.

approached the Sacraments more frequently; in a word, spared nothing to learn God's will, resolved to follow it, whatever might be the kind of life destined by Providence for him. After he had persevered for some time in these fervent practices, the Mother of God appeared to him and said—"Tancred, you ask me to point out a state in which you can secure your salvation. Leave the world; a Religious Order, consecrated to my glory, will be for you the port of safety. Have confidence." At these words she vanished. The following night he saw, in a dream, two Religious of the Order of St. Dominic, the elder of whom, approaching, said to him in a mild tone—"You besought God, through the intercession of the Blessed Virgin, to instruct you how best to save your soul: rise promptly, you must pass the remainder of your life with us."

The next morning, when this young man was going to hear Mass, he met the Prior of the Dominicans of Bologna, and having looked at him attentively, he recognized him as the person he had beheld in his sleep. Surprised at this coincidence, he accosts him, relates what had happened. Then, no longer doubtful of God's will, he renounces all the advantages that may await him in the world and consecrates himself to God in the Order of Preachers, and crowned a holy life by a still holier death.*

So clear a revelation of God's designs regarding their choice of a state of life must not be looked for by all; but all may be certain that if they pray fervently to Mary, she will make known the divine will through the voice of those who direct them.

* Letourneur.

TWENTIETH DAY.

YET ten days, and this month of benediction shall be over. Let us then redouble the zeal, fervour, vivacity of our petitions, during these latter days of grace, so as not to prepare for ourselves the regret of having allowed a period, in which we might have obtained everything, to pass without fruit.

THE HOLY NAME OF MARY.

"*And the Virgin's name was Mary*" (St. Luke i. 27).

THERE is nothing in Mary, not even her name, which is not productive of light, grace, and salvation. Wonderful is this name, magnificent and all-powerful; a fertile channel of graces to those who invoke it with tender affection; to those who hold it in veneration and pronounce it with respect, it is a lively source of consolation. All find in it a remedy in misfortune, a treasury out of which to enrich themselves, and a beacon pointing out the road to eternal life. It is terrible to hell; crushes the serpent's head, and achieves signal victories over the prince of darkness.

Holy Virgin, as your Divine Son is styled *Admirable, Angel of the Council, Mighty God, Prince of the world to come, Prince of Peace*, so may your name be expatiated on by interpretations apposite to it. It is said to signify *Our Lady*, and in becoming Mother of God you were made Mistress of all creation. It is interpreted *Bitter sea*, and during the Passion of your Divine Son, your soul was transfixed with the sword of sorrows foretold by

Simeon. *Illuminatrix*, and you are the guide of poor sinners along the pilgrimage of life, bringing back the wanderers to the right path.

"Your name, O Mary," cries out St. Bernard, "like that of Jesus, is joy to the heart, honey to the mouth, melody to the ear. No, after that of Jesus, there is no other name upon earth, or in Heaven, so prolific of grace and hope to pious souls. The name of Mary contains within it a sweet and divine perfume; when it enters a friendly heart, it diffuses a delightful odour; and such is the property of this admirable name, that though repeated a thousand times it is ever new."

"O Virgin, sublime, compassionate, and worthy of all praise, your name cannot be uttered without inflaming the heart; the bare recollection of it recreates the minds of your servants."* "O Mary, the thought of your name imparts joy to the afflicted, brings back the wandering sheep to the way of salvation, and restores hope to the sinner."† It is preferable to earthly riches, for it dilates hearts contracted by the sorrows of life. "The glory of your name, O Mary, is likened to oil poured out, because oil diffuses a sweet odour and feeds the flame."‡ "Make the trial, O sinner! call upon the name of Mary, it alone suffices to heal your infirmities; nor is there any contagion so malignant as not to yield at once to the salutary influence of this name." §

In fine, your name, O Mother of God, is replete with grace and benediction; it cannot be pronounced without profit to the soul. "The virtue of this name is such that it softens the most obstinate

---

* St. Bernard.   † Laud.
‡ Richard of St. Laurence.   § *Ibid.*

heart." "It is a delicious perfume. May the odour which exhales divine grace be secreted within our innermost heart, as within a vase well prepared, and thence shed around its salutary emanations." "May Christians be mindful frequently to invoke, with confidence and love, a name which is for them a superabounding source of grace in this life and sublime glory in the next."* "Whoever will invoke your name," said our Saviour to His Blessed Mother in presence of St. Bridget, "and trusting in you will firmly resolve to amend his life, I will give three things—contrition for his sins, the means of satisfying My justice, strength to persevere, and finally the Kingdom of Heaven." "My brethren," said the venerable Thomas à Kempis, "if you desire to be comforted in your tribulations, go to Mary, pay her your homage, invoke her, recommend yourself to her. Rejoice with Mary, weep with Mary, walk with Mary, seek Jesus with Mary. Finally, desire to live with Jesus and Mary."

Practice.—Thrice daily, the children of the Church and of Mary are accustomed, all the world over, to do homage to that source and principle of their happiness, the Mystery of the Incarnation, by the recital of the *Angelus.* But, how often has it occurred to you, in acquitting yourself of this practice, to make it an act of thanksgiving to Jesus and Mary, for that immense benefit? Oh, had you done this, had you heartily besought Mary, every time you recited it, to enable you to penetrate the depths of this mystery of love, what light would have been imparted to you! what treasures of grace would now enrich your soul!

* St. Ligouri.

Aspiration.—" Mary ! O name, under whose invocation no one can be lost, be ever on my lips, ever present to my mind." *

Example.

A native of Germany committed a grievous sin ; shame prevented him from confessing it, and not being able to endure remorse of conscience, he resolved to drown himself, but arrived at the river, he dared not do it ; he wept scalding tears and prayed God to pardon him without confession. One night he felt himself struck on the shoulders, and heard a voice tell him—" Go to confession." He went to the church, but did not confess. He heard the same voice another night ; he returned to the church, but no sooner entered it than he said to himself—" I would rather die than confess this sin." He was going home, when it struck him to recommend himself first to the Blessed Virgin. Scarcely had he knelt down, than he felt himself changed. He asked for a confessor, made an avowal of his sins, shedding torrents of tears. He afterwards acknowledged that in this action he experienced more satisfaction than if he had gained all the gold of the universe.†

* St. Bernard.   † Auriemna, bk. iii., chap. 7.

TWENTY-FIRST DAY.

ON THE IMMACULATE HEART OF MARY.

"Him that cometh to me I will not cast out" (St. John vi. 37).

IF God has created amongst His Saints, hearts so tender, so noble, so generous, so compassionate, that those words of Job could be applied to them—" From my infancy mercy grew with me;"* what did He not do when fashioning the Heart of Mary? What treasures of goodness, mercy, and love has He not lavished on this Heart? What can we say, how find terms in which to extol the compassion, the tenderness of the Heart of Mary our Mother, the Mother of our God? *Quibus te laudibus efferam nescio.*† No, after the Heart of Jesus, you will not find a heart on earth or in Heaven so constantly open to you, none that takes so lively an interest in your salvation, which so tenderly compassionates your sufferings, enters so intimately into your joys and sorrows. The Heart of Mary is the heart of a mother, but of a Mother incomparably more tender and devoted than you can even imagine. It is the living image of the Heart of Jesus, Who was pleased to imprint in it all the movements, all the feelings with which He was Himself animated. It is into Mary's Heart that Jesus has cast without measure that divine fire which exhausted and consumed Himself for the souls He had come to save. Unite then, if you will, all the burning ardour created hearts have ever entertained for

* Job xxxi. 18.   † St. Augustine.

one another, all the flames that have consumed the Saints most inflamed with love for God and their neighbour; all these flames together are but *ice* compared with the love of the Heart of Mary for you. Like that of Jesus, this Heart is ever ready to assist you, ever as present to you, as if all its affections were concentrated in you alone. Nothing can distract or turn it aside from that one design—your eternal welfare; and at whatever hour you recur to it, you will find it occupied about you. Ah! love invokes love, heart calls on heart. Since you are so much loved, love you in return; for Mary makes but one request—that we sometimes call to mind, that we believe, this incomprehensible love; and if we think, if we put faith in it, we who are so tender towards those who love us, can we refuse to give her our confidence, our love, our heart?

Run then, Christians, all, run to the Heart of your Mother; it will not reject the child that comes to it. It can compassionate our miseries, for it is the Heart of the *Queen of Martyrs*, which at the foot of the Cross endured within it all sorrows, exhausted all bitterness. It will pour oil upon the wounds of our souls and bodies, for it is the *Health of the Sick*. It will be our asylum, our sanctuary in perils, temptations, afflictions, abandonment of creatures, for it is the *Help of Christians*. What do you fear? Where besides will you find a heart so tender, so powerful, so gracious? You have offended Mary by sinning against her Divine Son, and her Heart pardons you. You have been unmindful of it; never did it lose sight of you. You have wandered far away from the fold of the Divine Pastor; the Heart of your Mother pursued, harassed you incessantly, with remorse. You closed your heart to the impressions of grace; it kept at the door and knocked, and by that gentle violence, which has roused so many sinners from the sleep of eternal death, it effected an entrance as though in spite of you, and restored you to life.

Be mindful, therefore, of this excess of love; never lose the remembrance of it, and endeavour to repay it by the most solid devotion and lively gratitude.

Practice.—Our heart created to be the sanctuary of the Divinity, becomes too frequently the abode of the enemy; faults, or at least numerous infidelities, tarnish its lustre. For this reason the Saints, jealous of this interior beauty, which charms the Heart of God, endeavoured to regain it by daily confession. You cannot imitate them in this point, but every evening, after your examen, confess to Mary, as the Church herself teaches—"I confess to Blessed Mary ever Virgin." This tender Mother, whom one of the holy Fathers styles "Sacerdotal Virgin," will doubtless obtain for you, together with contrition, the remission of those slight faults you will have accused yourself of to her. If you have had the misfortune to sin mortally, this act of filial confidence will merit for you the grace of promptly coming forth from that sad state, by a good and fervent sacramental confession.

Aspiration.—O most loving Heart of Mary, take possession of our hearts both in time and in eternity!

Example.

On Sunday, 15th February, 1857, the Confraternity of our Lady of Chartres was celebrating its Patronal Feast, and the thirtieth anniversary of its consecration to the Immaculate Heart of Mary. This twofold circumstance brought to all the Offices a large concourse of people, and especially in the evening at the solemn hour of the recommendations, every avenue leading to the chapel of the pilgrimage was beset by a vast and recollected crowd, eager to hear the touching requests forwarded from all parts of the diocese, and even of all France, and which express such confidence in our Lady of Chartres. Among other favours demanded of Mary, her maternal solicitude was invoked in behalf of a little orphan of five; the petition was framed in the following terms—" The prayers of the confraternity are earnestly requested for a little girl of five, who has just lost her mother, to the end that our Lady of Chartres may take her under her holy protection, and may inspire some charitable soul to complete in her what was so well begun by her mother." Now, who can help admiring here the goodness of her none ever invoked in vain? At this confident appeal to our Lady of Chartres, a generous inspiration from Mary descended into the heart of one of the congregation, who immediately said to herself—" For the love of Mary, our common Mother, I will be that charitable soul. I will be a mother to this child who has no longer one."

So far all had passed in the secret of the sanctuary between the Immaculate Virgin and her faithful servant. What then were our surprise and delight when, the ceremony ended, the person disclosed to us the pious project, formed at the foot of the miraculous pillar of Mary.

On inquiry we learned that the orphan belonged to a poor but honest family of Viabon. To make known to the Curé the happy lot in reserve for his youthful parishioner, and send to Chartres this new child of Mary, was the work of some days. Received with open arms by her protectress, the poor child found in her a mother in every sense of the word.

By a refinement of modesty, that enhances still more the merit of the charity, the generous benefactress to whom Mary has confided the sweet mission of acting the part of mother to this child, imposed but one condition to her goodness, namely, that her secret be not divulged, but that our Lady of Chartres be left all the honour of an adoption which is her work. It may, however, be said without indiscretion, that the little girl was immediately placed at one of the best schools in the town, there to receive a Christian education. Perhaps the most striking and most consoling feature in the case is, that everybody who had known the mother, regards it as a manifest recompense of her tender devotion to Mary. On this head she was a real subject of edification to the whole parish in which she resided; and she had nothing so much at heart as to implant similar sentiments in her child. Moved by a concurrence of circumstances so evidently providential, a large number of the inhabitants of Viabon, headed by the Curé, have hastened to get themselves enrolled in the Confraternity of our Lady of Chartres, thus to perpetuate among them a *souvenir* that entitles them to rely in all things on the kindness of the Heart of Mary.

Previous to her arrival at Chartres, our little orphan was called " Aimée;" now she is universally recognized as " Aimée de Marie," a name which Mary herself will doubtless glory in ratifying, by continuing in favour of her adopted child the maternal protection, whose salutary effects she has already experienced in so remarkable a manner.*

* L.'Abbé Legendre.

TWENTY-SECOND DAY.

IMMACULATE CONCEPTION OF MARY—SUBLIME SANCTITY TO WHICH SHE WAS ELECTED.

" *The Most High hath sanctified His tabernacle*" (Psalm xlv. 5).

MARY was conceived without sin, that is to say, that, from the first moment of her existence, she presented herself to the eyes of God pure and spotless, and in virtue of the foreknown merits of her Divine Son, exempt from original guilt. Of all the children of Adam she alone could say—"'The Lord possessed me in the beginning of my ways.'* His love entered my soul with life; never did He reckon me among those who have outraged His divine bounty." And only to Mary could God say—"'Thou art all fair, O My beloved, and there is not a spot in thee.'† 'As the lily among thorns, so art thou' among My other creatures."‡

To the children of Mary, zealous to revere, to honour above all her other privileges, that of her Immaculate Conception, we shall not stop to prove how just and meet it was that the dwelling of the Most High should never have been for a single day the abode of His enemy; that the *Mother of God* should never have been the enemy of her God; that the *Terror of the demon*, she who was to crush his head, should never for one instant have owned his sway; that the *Mediatrix* of the human race should not have shared in the universal prevarication; that the *Queen of Angels*, created and

---

* Prov. viii. 22. † Cant. iv. 7. ‡ Cant. ii. 2.

M

preserved in innocence, should herself be pure and unspotted.

Besides, after the glorious Definition of the 8th of December, 1854, the children of Mary have no more to do to defend their Mother's honour, they have but to felicitate her and congratulate themselves, repeating with transports of joy—"*Rome has spoken, the cause is ended; Glory be to God, glory be to Mary!*"

What immeasurable torrents of grace were poured into Mary's soul, to what degree of holiness and love did she attain, in virtue and by consequence of this unique and incomparable privilege which prepared her for the divine Maternity! We shall never be able to comprehend it in this life. God is admirable in His Saints. He bent down towards them with inconceivable condescension, treated them with surprising familiarity, made them participate in His riches, so as to render them in some degree all-powerful; and when we read their own account of those favours, in as far as they have been able to describe them, it only remains for us to exclaim with the royal Prophet—" God is wonderful in His Saints. . . . To me Thy friends are exceedingly honourable, their principality is exceedingly strengthened."*

If already we are at a loss for terms in which to speak of the Saints, weak creatures, and conceived in iniquity, and who not unfrequently have added to the original stain so many grave and voluntary faults, how shall it be with us when we have to treat of Mary? It is an acknowledged maxim among theologians that there is no gift, no favour granted to the servants, but the Queen of Heaven

---

* Psalm cxxxviii. 17.

possessed it in its sublimest degree. When God created Mary, whom He destined to be His living and animated tabernacle, He began this work at a point surpassing the highest perfection attainable even by His elect; He created her in an innocence, in a perfection, a degree of love superior to that of the Seraphim themselves; and thence her lights, her ardours continually increased. What, therefore, shall we say of this Queen of Sanctity? "Of Mary we can never say enough." "Glorious things are spoken of thee, O city of God!" And yet how comes it that despite all the holy Fathers have endeavoured to reveal to us, your Heart is still unsatisfied? Ah! it is that your greatness, your perfection, the stupendous liberalities of God in your regard, O Mary, bring you so near to God Himself, that *silence* is our only fitting tribute of praise to exalt your sanctity; this holiness is a mystery of grandeur and humility, whose glory is inclosed in the bottom of your heart. "All the glory of the King's daughter is from within."* It is a secret which the King has reserved for Himself, and to the knowledge of which none but His most privileged servants are admitted; an abyss whose depths they may imperfectly sound in the stillness of prayer, but which it is neither allowable or possible for them to reveal. O Jesus, what do we but lisp when we attempt to speak of you, of your divine Mother? From the midst of our darkness, of our helplessness, we praise you, O Jesus, through Mary—Mary, we praise you through Jesus.

Practice.—Mary would have preferred exemption from that sad law by which we become enemies to God even before our birth, to the divine Maternity;

---

* Psalm xliv. 14.

hence she is pleased to reward her servants who zealously honour and exalt her Immaculate Conception. Among all her Feasts, let the 8th of December be with you a special day of devotion; act so that you may inspire others with a like confidence in your Immaculate Mother.

Aspiration.— O Mary, conceived without sin, pray for us who have recourse to you.

Example.

To have recourse to Mary in every necessity was a maxim which Blessed Alphonsus Rodriguez instilled into all with whom he came in contact: nor did he neglect any opportunity of pronouncing her eulogium and upholding her privileges. He honoured with special devotion the Immaculate Conception of the Queen of Virgins and her glorious Assumption into Heaven, the pious belief in which he defended with equal zeal and solidity, persuaded that the honour of the Mother and of the Son are alike involved in Mary's having been all pure from her Conception, and her virginal body being now glorified in Heaven. Mary seemed to take complacency in the ardour with which Alphonsus defended the interests of her glory. She twice commanded him to commit to writing all the prayers he was accustomed to address to her. On another occasion, she expressed to him how sensibly she felt herself honoured by his devotion to her Immaculate Conception, and inspired him with the firm resolution to be everywhere its panegyrist and apostle; so that Alphonsus, otherwise so reserved, became all on fire whenever this prerogative of Mary was in question. He declared openly, that to believe his Blessed Mother was conceived without stain, and to honour her in this quality, was a sure means of pleasing Jesus Christ. Not content with reciting the Office of the Immaculate Conception, he wrote copies of it, which he distributed among the students of the College, declaring that this prayer would be useful toward preserving purity of heart. He feared not even to say that the Society of Jesus was founded partly in order to defend and propagate this Devotion, adding that if the Father Rector permitted him, he would go and preach it in the streets and public places; in fine, hearing two Fathers one day debating this question, he drew near, and taking part in the conversation, said, in a confident tone—" I know the Mother of God was conceived without original sin." "And from whom did you learn it?" asked one of the Fathers. "From Mary herself," was the reply.

The Blessed Virgin was pleased to testify her appreciation of Alphonsus' zeal by a marvellous prodigy. In the year 1586, the Feast of the Immaculate Conception was celebrated at Majorca with much pomp. The same day, a hurricane, such as occasionally devastates the Antilles, suddenly burst over the city; and such was the violence of wind, that on all sides were heard lamentations and wailings, in the anticipation of the most terrible accidents. One of the College walls had just fallen, burying several persons beneath its ruins. As more serious disasters were apprehended, the Religious hastened to leave the house, which might be destroyed at any moment. Father Rector, perceiving Alphonsus behind him, going away with the others, said to him, "What brings you here, Brother? Go quickly to the church, and deprecate the anger of the Lord." Alphonsus obeyed, and he had scarcely bent his knees before the altar, when the storm suddenly sudsided, so that they were in time to draw forth from beneath the ruins those whom they had deemed victims of this fearful disaster.*

* *Life of Blessed Alphonsus Rodriguez.*

TWENTY-THIRD DAY.

MARY TEACHES HER SERVANTS HOW TO PRAY.

"Ah!" Mother, "behold, I cannot speak" to you, or to your Son, "for I am a child" (Jer. i. 6).

THE grand, the only secret of the spiritual life is prayer, by the aid of which, were we deprived of all other helps, we are sure of salvation. Prayer is always within my reach; chains, illness, persecution may deprive me of the Sacraments; I cannot every hour apply to these great means of salvation and life; but in whatever situation I may be, I can each instant, without even interrupting my occupations, descend into the oratory of my heart, and invoke that divine succour which the Lord has solemnly pledged Himself shall be granted to all who solicit it. "Amen, I say to you .... whatsoever you shall ask the Father in My name, that will I do."*

This invincible weapon, prayer, renders us strong against the devil, against our passions, against the Omnipotent Himself. What did that mysterious wrestle, in which the Angel vanquished by Jacob conferred upon him the name of Israel—strong against God—denote? The strength, the efficacy of prayer. If an angry Deity wills to be disarmed of His wrath, what does He inspire to nations, as well as to individuals? To pray. If He desires to make His arm weigh heavily, what does He do? He turns men from prayer; and such is the power of this means of salvation, that it seems as though

---

* St. John xiv. 12, 13.

He feared being prayed to; for when one of His servants pleaded with Him of old for an ungrateful and rebellious people, He said, "Let Me alone, that My wrath may be kindled against them, and that I may destroy them."* Moses persists, and notwithstanding His indignation, the Lord suffers Himself to be appeased. *Placatusque est Deus.*† Why, then, is prayer so powerful? It is because to pray is to humble yourself, to confess your impotency, to render the homage of your nothingness to the almightiness of God; and He has said, "A contrite and humble heart I will not despise;" a heart that, despairing of self, expects all from Me.

Of the power, the efficacy of prayer, we are fully convinced, Christians and children of Mary; but how often are we tempted to forget it, to give up this victorious weapon! Then it is that Mary comes to our aid; she smoothes the difficulties that discourage us; she herself inspires this spirit of prayer, of perseverance in prayer; she calms our imagination, and causes us to find in this holy exercise delights unknown to those who have not experienced them. Let our brethren led back to the fold by the hand of Mary tell us—What is the chief want of their heart, the first science in which Mary instructed them? Is it not prayer? And how may we go to Mary herself? What is the spell that draws her towards us? Prayer! Let us, then, pray, ever pray to Mary, pray through Mary, and never cease. Should our ingratitude, our unworthiness seal our lips in presence of the thrice holy God, of Whom we have contemned the benefits, outraged the power, let us venture to address Mary, let us always dare to invoke Mary;

---

* Exodus xxxii. 10.   † Exodus xxxii. 14.

should we have laid aside all other prayer, let us, as a last plank in shipwreck, pray to Mary; let us beware of yielding to the importunity of the enemy, who would fain snatch this plank from us; let us persist in supplication to Mary, and we shall escape the imminent danger which threatens us, and shall even have it in our power also to say—Blessed be the Lord Who hath given me to persevere in calling upon the name of Mary, and hath preserved me a place in her tender compassion!

Mary not alone teaches us how to pray, but she prays with and for us; there is not a sigh of our heart, an invocation of our mouth, but elicits a prayer from our Mother in Heaven. Faith imparts to us this consoling truth, private revelations confirm it. One day, whilst they sang at Mass these words, *Ora Virgo*—" Pray, O Virgin," St. Gertrude saw Mary turn towards her Son with a suppliant look, her hands joined, in order to beseech Him in favour of those who were invoking her on earth; and forthwith our Lord blessed all these souls by forming the sign of the Cross over them. On another occasion, at the verse, *Audi nos*—" Hear us," Mary appeared to the same Saint, seated on a very lofty throne, and Gertrude having said to her —" Why, O Mother of Mercy, why do you not pray for us?" the Blessed Virgin replied—" I speak for you with all my Heart to the Heart of my beloved Son."

O Mary! you are the only one whose lamp was never extinguished during the night of this life. Your Heart ever beat in response to the loving Heart of your Divine Son; the hours of rest even interrupted not your prayer, and you could truly say, " I sleep, but my heart watcheth "—*Ego dormio et cor meum vigilat.* On the contrary, what are our prayers? A spiritual slumber hardly intermitted by a few turnings to God. Alas! my Mother, I cannot speak to you or your Son—*A. a. a. nescio loqui.** Open then my mouth—*Aperi os meum*, teach me to praise you; and should I be incapable thereof, speak to me yourself, speak, pray, implore for me! Teach me to hear your voice, the voice of your inspirations, and to follow it with inviolable fidelity.

Practice.—We usually pray without preparation, consequently without fruit. We shall not find strength in this holy exercise, if we are not resolved to apply to it as seriously as to a temporal affair, the success of which we have really at heart.

1. *Banish resolutely every idea foreign to our prayer.* "Worldly solicitudes, thoughts of temporal affairs, remain here," St. Bernard used to say when taking holy water; "come not to distract me in this holy place, I will resume you at my departure hence."

2. *Be sorry for faults committed*, which raise, as it were, a wall of separation between God and us.

3. *Impress ourselves with a lively sense of the presence of God;* ask the grace to make our prayer well; invariably begin prayer by calling on Mary, that she may be as a rampart around our soul.

Aspiration.—Mary, teach us to pray!—*Doce nos orare.*

Example.

Magdalen Morice—born the 31st July, 1736, and departed this life 17th March, 1769—was the daughter of a farmer in the diocese of St. Malo. From her earliest years she was led into paths of

* Jer. i. 6.

the most eminent sanctity, amid the laborious occupations of her mean condition. About the age of nine, having lost her father, to whom she was tenderly attached, she could not be consoled till the Blessed Virgin, to whom she had a singular devotion, came herself to alleviate her sorrow. The following is Magdalen's account of the occurrence as inserted in her Life, which she wrote under obedience—" I had not yet made the sacrifice of my father, when one morning, as I was engaged keeping the sheep on a heath, I gave way more than ever to grief, and flinging myself on the ground, I wept very bitterly. A lady just then passed, observed my trouble, and drawing near, said with an air of mingled gravity and sweetness, ' What is the matter, my child, that you weep so? Tell me the cause of your grief.' ' I am weeping, madam, for the death of my father,' I replied. She asked me if he were long dead? I told her about six days. 'It is time, my child,' rejoined she, 'to make the sacrifice of him.' 'Ah, madam, I wish I could make it, but I have not the courage.' 'My daughter, do you not daily say the "Our Father"? Do you not say, "Thy will be done"? Think, my child, that it is God's will that has bereft you of your father, He desires Himself to hold the place of parent to you. Say then now, My Father is in Heaven! Cast yourself into His arms, address Him with confidence. I promise you that this Father will take greater care of you than the father you have lost ever did.' Her words awoke a feeling of consolation within me, I made willingly at the moment—what I had not been able to resolve on doing for six days—the sacrifice of my father. But I felt myself suddenly so attached to this good lady, that I could have wished her to remain with me for ever. Her presence inspired me with such delicious feelings, imparted so much consolation to me, that I felt quite changed. My heart became wholly inflamed with the love of God; I burned with the desire of pleasing Him. To detain this lady, and thus enjoy her presence, I said to her: 'Madam, there is something in the "Our Father" which I cannot comprehend; will you have the goodness to explain it to me? When I say—"Thy kingdom come," of what kingdom do I speak? Can I hope to obtain it?' A sweet smile lit up the features of the good lady, and she said in a tone of kindness—'That kingdom belongs to the Master of consummate felicity; this Master is your Father; this Father loves you tenderly: why then should you not be entitled to His kingdom? But, as an aspirant to this kingdom, my child, you must attach yourself to the service of God, seeking to please Him alone.' 'Ah! Madam,' I said, 'to serve this good Master is my only desire; but I do not know the way to reach this beautiful kingdom of which you speak; will you have the goodness to show it me?' 'You have a long road to travel,' she answered, 'and this road is termed the "Way of the Cross;" beware of seeking to withdraw from it; it is the most secure, leading directly to the kingdom you are inquiring after. You shall have much to suffer, my child; but take courage. Let it sink deep into your mind, that your sufferings are only permitted for God's glory and your own advantage. Nothing shall befall you except at His command; He will sustain you, and proportion His graces to your trials.' 'Madam,' I said, 'to undertake the journey you have traced for me, I must previously enter on the path of virtue; I feel my weakness, I am too blind to lead myself, yet I have no guide.' She began to smile, saying—' Leave yourself to Providence. It will send you a guide; be docile.' She then presented me with a little image of the Blessed Virgin, which she had with her, saying—' Remember me; be faithful to grace.' I felt quite beside myself, and remained for a moment without consciousness. On returning to myself, I no longer found my good lady; this grieved me, but I recollected what she had told me, that nothing should happen to me, but by the command of God. I immediately returned home much comforted, and resolved to love God, to attach myself to Him alone, to seek to please Him, cost what it might. I was careful not to display the gift I had received from the lady, but hid it as best I could in my bed; and my greatest pleasure was to shut myself up in my cell with this statue, and many were the consolations I tasted there. I called it my Good Mother, to salute it, telling it that as long as I lived I would recite the little chaplet called 'The Crown of the Holy Virgin.' This little prayer has been of great benefit to me. I passed many a night before my little statue, and would have passed many more, had not God sent me a guide, who, on learning my manner of life, thought proper to retrench many of my practices. It was certainly Providence led me under the care of a director so prudent and virtuous."*

* *Life of the Ecstatica of Brittany, Magdalen Monica.*

TWENTY-FOURTH DAY.

MARY CONDUCTS US TO JESUS.

" We would see Jesus," we would love Jesus: lead us to Him, O Mary (St. John xii. 21).

JESUS is the beginning, the middle, and the end of our beatitude, as well in this life as in the other. Our heart was formed for Him; it is for Him it is unconsciously calling out, when recoiling from creatures in disgust, and weary of the profound void left by created objects, it proceeds anew to cry out for happiness.

O human heart, immense capacity of God! When is it, O man! that, even though laden with goods, with honours, surrounded with the fondest affection, you never say, " It is enough?" Why ever seek after, ever asking for new enjoyments from all that surround you? What is wanting to you? God, Whom the likeness engraved on your soul ever calls for; God, Whose image you reflect; and *all*, with Him is wanting.

O men! how have you wandered away; you are running hungry, thirsty, in the very midst of abundance. "I ran in thirst."* Who will place you again on the right track? How shall you find Him again—that God, your fulness, your only beatitude—living, as you have so long been, in oblivion of, and indifference to, Him? Who shall draw aside the veils that conceal this ravishing Beauty, towards Whom you would rush with irresistible impetuosity, could you but perceive

* Psalm lxi. 5.

His amiabilities, His perfections? Have recourse to Mary; no one cometh to the Father unless drawn by the Son, and no one comes to the Son unless Mary attracts him. Vainly would you call, seek, try to revivify Him in your heart, if you do not seek Him in Mary, if this Divine Mother comes not to aid your pursuit. Mary is the celestial field in which this precious pearl lies hid; she has a sort of propriety over her Son, Who is entirely her own; and in virtue of this right, so eminent, so sublime, she has a special power of bestowing Jesus on souls. Thus, St. Francis of Assisium, commenting on these words of St. Matthew—" They found the Child with Mary His Mother," goes so far as to say—" You seek Jesus in vain, if you seek Him not with Mary and through Mary." "Ah!" said St. Ildefonsus, in a like sentiment, " I wish to become the servant of Mary, in order to become the servant of Jesus." You, then, whom the Spirit of Love has inspired with desire to reach the Son, separate not from His Mother in the pursuit; entreat her to extend to you a helping hand, to accompany you in your researches. For should she desert you, you are sure to stray—never shall you attain the goal. But if you adhere inseparably to Mary, she will enkindle in your heart a spark of that divine fire which burned in her own; she will penetrate your soul with that salutary bitterness which filled hers during those days she herself was seeking her Divine Child, Who, to try His Mother, and encourage us under abandonment, was pleased to withdraw from her sweet society; and through Mary, with Mary, how could you fail to find Jesus? Cast yourself into the arms of this incomparable Mother, and, touched by the desires she herself has excited in your heart, she will show you, will accustom you to study in her own Heart, Him that is all good—*Ostendam tibi omne bonum;* Him, that is the complement of every good—*Omne delectamentum in se habentem.* She will cause you to know Him, not as our feeble intelligence can conceive, but as she herself knows Him, replete with every charm calculated to win our hearts.

Ah, Jesus! that Treasure which for thirty-three years Mary possessed visibly, which she kept enshrined in heart so long as she dwelt upon earth, all she asks is to make Him known, to communicate Him to souls. This is the aim of all the wonders she effects; it is not solely on her own account she desires the conquest of our hearts: it is to offer them to the Heart of Jesus, to Whom she gave her own Heart with its every affection, its every motion. Some, actuated by a laudable zeal for the divine honour, others by a counterfeit zeal, appear to dread lest we carry veneration to Mary beyond due bounds, and forget the Son for the Mother. But let both parties be reassured: Mary has the art of referring to Jesus the homage rendered to herself; she knows how to turn to Him the hearts of her children; and we have not one example of a really devout client of Mary remaining for a long time indifferent to Jesus. Nor could Jesus feel jealous of the honours paid to His Mother, for He receives them as though they were addressed to Himself. This He expressly testified to His faithful servant St. Gertrude. One day as the Antiphon, "Thou art all fair"—*Quam pulchra es!* was being chanted, the Saint addressed it to Mary in the name of her Divine Son. Our most loving Lord received this homage with benign sweetness, and bowing His head in thanksgiving, said to St. Gertrude—" I will at a fitting time repay with royal magnificence and divine liberality, this honour which you have paid in My Person to My sweetest Mother."*

What God has joined let no one separate—Jesus and Mary ; let both live and reign in our heart, and it shall experience even amidst the trials and afflictions of life that peace which surpasses all understanding—all consolation ; that peace which God alone can infuse into the soul, which the world cannot give ; and we shall be able to cry out with St. Augustine—" Oh ! how delightful has the finding of You, O my God, rendered the privation of those trifles I so much dreaded to lose ! "

Practice.—What is life throughout, but the cry of the Christian soul to its God, beseeching Him to succour it, never to leave it alone ? Let your first want, your first movement on awaking be, to seek your God, to cast yourself into His arms. Rejecting all other preoccupation, say to Him every morning with renewed fervour—"' Lord, my heart hath sought Thee. Thy face, O Lord, I will still seek ; turn not away Thy face from me.'† Deign, O Lord, to keep me this day in Your love ; this I beg in the name of Mary." On this action well made, depends, generally speaking, the entire day.

Aspiration.—O Mary ! Jesus my Lord and my God is with you ! He is yours, do not refuse me; give Him to my soul, that ardently longs for Him !

Example.

In a village at a short distance from Florence, lived a maiden named Dominica, the offspring of

---

* Bk. iv., chap. iii.   † Psalm xxvi. 8, 9.

poor parents. From her infancy she was devout to our Blessed Lady, fasted daily in her honour; on Saturday she distributed to the poor the nourishment of which she had deprived herself; she gathered in her garden, or in the adjacent fields, all the flowers she could, and presented them to a statue of the Holy Virgin holding the Divine Infant in her arm. Mary in return visited this child with the most distinguished favours. When Dominica had attained her tenth year, happening one day to be at the window, she saw in the street a female of noble bearing, accompanied by a charming little child; both held out their hands as if imploring an alms. She at once went to get them some bread; but before she could open the door, they were at her side, and she perceived that the child's hands, feet, and side, were wounded. "Ah," said Dominica, "who has wounded this boy?" "Love," the mother replied. Charmed with his beauty and modesty, Dominica asked him if his wounds were painful. His only answer was a smile. As they were standing near the statue of Jesus and Mary, the mother said to Dominica—"Tell me, child, why do you crown the images with flowers?" "It is," she replied, "the love I bear to Jesus and Mary." "And do you love them much?" "As much as I can." "How much is that?" "As much as grace enables me." "Continue," said the mother, "continue to love them; they will know how to reward you in Paradise." A celestial odour issuing from the wounds of the child, Dominica asked the mother, what ointment she was accustomed to dress them with, and whether it could be bought. "It may be purchased by faith and good works," she replied. Dominica offered them some bread.

"My son's food," resumed the mother, "is love; tell him you love Jesus, and he will be content." At these words the child became quite joyous, and turning to Dominica asked her how much she loved Jesus. "How much do I love Him?" rejoined she. "I love Him so much, that day and night I never cease thinking of Him; my sole desire is to know how to please Him." "Well," replied the child, "love Him, and love will teach you how to please Him." The perfume of his wounds continuing to augment, Dominica cried out—"My God, this perfume makes me die of love! If so delicious the odour a child can exhale, what must the odour of Paradise be!" But on a sudden a bright light surrounded the Mother, and she appeared robed as a Queen, the Child shone as the sun. He took the flowers with which Dominica had adorned His image, and strewed them over the head of the pious girl, who, recognizing in these august personages *Jesus* and *Mary*, had flung herself at their feet. Thus ended the vision. Dominica afterwards took the habit of St. Dominic, and died in the odour of sanctity, A.D. 1558.*

* St. Ligouri.

TWENTY-FIFTH DAY.

TOKENS WHEREBY WE MAY DISCOVER IF WE LOVE MARY.

"*I wish to love Mary*" (Blessed Berchmans).

DEVOTION to Mary being so efficacious, so indispensable a means of salvation, it imports us—be our desire of eternal bliss ever so faint—to make sure we are possessed of this treasure, that we are marked with this sign of predestination. Let us examine what are the characteristics of sincere friends, of devoted hearts. He that loves thinks unceasingly on the beloved— not for an instant is she out of his sight. Her name ever hovers on his lips; to converse with her is the charm of his life; he cannot bear her absence; the most painful sacrifices are light to prove his affection. The property of love is communication of goods, and to take upon oneself the sufferings of the beloved. Love finds us like, or assimilates us; it takes the tastes and ideas of the object loved, imitates her, gives her himself, and to the gift of himself would, if possible, add that of the universe.

You love Mary, then, if you think often of her; if you take pleasure in speaking of her, in hearing her praises; if you rejoice at the honour rendered her by others, the prodigies which daily increase her fame. You love Mary if her name, with that of Jesus, is the first that rises to your lips on awaking, the last you utter before retiring to rest, and if it remains in the depth of your heart as a permanent remembrance, an incessant prayer. You love Mary if you celebrate her Feasts with fervour, if you pass no day without visiting, without praying to her; if you inspire your dependents or others with her love, or desire to do so. You love Mary if, not satisfied in sharing in her joys, you enter especially into her sorrows—if you love to meditate on them, contrive to impose some sacrifice on yourself in memory of those she endured for you. Lastly, and above all, you love Mary if you seek to make your life a living and faithful copy of hers; if you love, as she did, prayer, solitude, labour; if you detest what she detested, shun what she shunned; if you practise the virtues that shone in her—humility, purity, abandonment to the divine will.

"Alas!" it will be said, "if such be the true servant of Mary, if such the characteristics by which her lovers are recognized, then must I confess that her love is very faint—hardly exists in my heart." Ah! do not lose courage. Do you not at least wish to have this desire? Do you not long to feel those lively ardours that consume the hearts of her true servants? Are you not grieved at seeing yourself so tepid, so cold in her love? Yes, doubtless. Then already has Mary visited your heart, already you have begun to love her; her love is not extinct in your soul, yet a little while and you will love her perfectly.

To attain this desired end you know all that is requisite; only put your hand to the work, try and do what is in your power—Mary will accomplish the rest. You will wonder to see the facility with which obstacles are overcome, and with what goodness and condescension she draws nigh to those who seek her. Oh, how promptly, how wisely, would you be instructed in her school. A glance of hers suffices to change hearts, to attach them irrevocably to her love. She said not a word to that happy Israelite (Père Ratisbonne), brought back in our own days to the faith of that Messiah expected by his fathers, *but at her feet he understood all*—all religion, all its mysteries. His heart burned within him like those of the Disciples of Emmaus, and he felt so raised above himself and the world as to find courage to make the most generous sacrifices.

If Mary operates not in our behalf one of those dazzling miracles which illumine souls and transform them in an instant—one of those miracles which we must admire, for which we can never praise her too highly, but which our weakness, and the self-love always alive in us, must not permit us to envy or solicit; she has still in her treasury graces—secret, powerful, and safe—for us, graces which lead the soul step by step to her Son, which confirm it daily more and more in His love. And these graces she dispenses with no niggard hand, but pours them with profusion on her devoted clients. Only try it, and you too shall be able to apprize others, through that conviction of the heart which alone possesses the secret of persuading, what marvels a solid and abiding devotion to Mary effects in the soul. "*Come and I will relate to you what she hath done for my soul.*"*

Practice.—The lover bestows on those dear to the beloved some of the affection which he has given to the cherished object of his heart. Therefore do you love, entertain a special devotion for those Saints most distinguished for love of Mary— St. John Evangelist, St. Bernard, St. Dominic, St. Ignatius, St. Ligouri. But above all have Alphonsus'

* Psalm cxvii.

particular devotion to her holy parents, St. Joachim and St. Anne, also to her glorious spouse St. Joseph. "I know not," says St. Teresa, "how any one can think of the Queen of Angels, and on the care she bestowed on Jesus in His childhood, without thanking St. Joseph for the assistance he rendered during that period to both Son and Mother." Then she adds—"I never knew any person having a special devotion to him but made sensible progress in virtue, nor do I remember ever having preferred a request to him that was not granted."

Aspiration.—Mary my Mother! Would that I could love you as your devoted servants have loved you, as the Angels love, even as your Divine Son Himself loves you.

Example.

St. Bernardine, of the Order of Friars Minor, was born at Massa, of which his father was Governor, on the Feast of the Nativity of the Blessed Virgin, 1380. This same Festival he subsequently selected to take the habit of St. Francis, make his profession, preach his first sermon, and say his first Mass. His parents, who had obtained him through the intercession of the Mother of God, were early taken away from him, and the child was received by a relative, who remarked even then, with admiration, indications of uncommon sanctity in him.

She often beheld him prostrate before an image of the Blessed Virgin, melting into tears as he repeated the "Hail Mary" with the fervour of an Angel, for, night and day, all Bernardine's supplications, whatever prayers he poured forth, were addressed to Mary, Mother of Jesus. From his tenderest years he fasted in her honour every Saturday, and during his whole life he never laid this practice aside.

Nevertheless, his pious relative, seeing Bernardine so young and comely, feared the loss of his innocence of soul and body. To preserve this treasure to him, many were the prayers she addressed to God and the Blessed Virgin, nor did she fail to warn him of the dangers of the world. He replied—"I am already smitten with love, and it would be my death were I to pass a day without visiting my beloved." Often he added—"I am going to see my beloved, who is beautiful beyond all the daughters of Sienna." Surmounting the gate of Sienna which leads to Florence, was a statue of the Holy Virgin; twice a day—morning and evening—Bernardine was accustomed to visit it, and there devoutly offer up his prayers. It is of this he spoke when he said—"I could not sleep at night, if the preceding day I was unable to see the image of my beloved."

In order to relieve her anxiety, his relative watched him for several successive days at the hour he was wont to say—"I am going to visit my beloved." She saw him several time stop before the statue of the Blessed Virgin, place himself on his knees, and pray with the utmost devotion, then rising, return straight home. His pious aunt, seeing all her apprehensions turned to spiritual consolations, wished, however, to sound the disposition of Bernardine. "My dear child," she said, one day, "I pray you keep me no longer in suspense; tell me on whom you have placed your affections, in order that, if she be of suitable rank, we may procure you her hand." Bernardine replied—"Since you enjoin me I will reveal to you the secret of my heart. I love the Holy Virgin, Mother of God, whom I have ever loved, whom I earnestly desire to behold, to whom I am betrothed as to a most chaste spouse, in whom are centered all my hopes. It is she who is the sovereign object of my affections—she alone I seek, she whom I wish to contemplate unceasingly with due respect, but since it is not given me to do so in this life I have resolved daily to visit her statue. You now know the object of my love."*

And amply did Mary reward her faithful servant. She condescended to appear to him one day and to say—" Bernardine, your devotion pleases me. As a pledge of still greater rewards I endow you with the talent of preaching and the power of working miracles. These gifts I have obtained for you from my Divine Son, and I promise, in addition, to make you a participator in the eternal bliss I enjoy in Heaven." The event justified this promise. Bernardine, by his sermons, regenerated entire Italy, he illumined the Church by the light of his doctrine as he rejoiced it by the holiness of his life.

* Rohrbacher.

TWENTY-SIXTH DAY.

THE TRUE SERVANT OF MARY SHOULD CONDOLE WITH HER SORROWS.

"Forget not the groanings of your mother" (Ecclus. vii. 29).

JESUS has many friends to partake of His joys, His glory, His holy table, but He finds few to follow Him to the Cross on Calvary. Mary also finds many to share in her greatness and her triumph, who know how to avail themselves of the omnipotence with which she has been endowed, but she looks round in vain among those dear to her; she sees none to console her, not one to bear her company in her dolours—who loves to meditate thereon, who is pleased to suffer with her. And by this alone does she recognize her true children; see if you be of the number. She invites you in the following terms—" Child, forget not the groanings of your Mother! Recall the tears you have cost her."

Who shall recount the Dolours of Mary? Oh. to measure the extent, the continuity of these, one should be able to penetrate into her Heart, nay. into the Sacred Heart of Jesus Himself, since, in becoming His Mother, she associated herself in all Its anguish, all Its agony. O Virgin daughter of Sion! to whom shall I compare you? With whom shall I liken you? Your grief is great as the sea; your days, your nights, have passed in weeping. And what is the cause of this immeasureable grief? It is Jesus; it is the ignominies, the torments of His Passion, which you endure in your Heart—not alone during this night, this ever memorable day of His sufferings and death, which eternity will not suffice to meditate on and understand—but during the entire three-and-thirty years of His mortal career. O Mary! if to you it has been given to enter, on the day of your Assumption, more into the joy of the Lord than has been granted to any other creature ; if you entered the holy city leaning on your Divine Son Himself; ah! it is because, during your pilgrimage, you had received Him *dead* into your arms, you had entered more profoundly than any other into His sufferings. O Children of Mary, how much do we owe to our Mother for the life-long pangs she bore for us in the person of her Divine Son, for those which she underwent at the foot of the Cross in offering to God the death of Jesus for the salvation of all in general and each in particular! An Angel revealed to St. Bridget that this sacrifice was more intolerable to Mary than the combined pangs of all martyrdoms. Our Holy Mother complained personally to St. Bridget that "very few condoled with her in her sorrows, the greater number of persons living and dying without having ever given them a serious thought." Our Lord, Who delights in seeing His Mother honoured, said one day to Blessed Veronica de Binasco—" Precious in My sight are the tears shed in honour of My Passion ; but, as I love My Mother with an immense affection, I do not less esteem meditation on the Dolours she endured at My death."

Practice.—Impose on yourself the sweet obligation of meditating now and then on the Dolours of Mary ; occasionally recite the *Stabat Mater*, that touching hymn of a soul deeply sensible of Mary's anguish. It was revealed to St. Elizabeth, a Benedictine Religious, that our Lord has promised four special graces to those who cherish devotion to the Dolours of Mary. (1) That whoever will invoke her through her Dolours shall do penance before death. (2) The Lord will comfort him in his tribulations, especially those of his last hour. (3) Jesus will imprint His Passion in his mind and heart. (4) Mary herself shall obtain whatever graces she desires in favour of those devoted to her Dolours.

Aspiration.—

> O thou Mother, fount of love,
> Touch my spirit from above,
> Make my heart with thine accord!

Example.

Blessed Joachim Piccolomini, celebrated for his tender devotion to Mary, contracted, from childhood, the habit of visiting thrice daily an image of our Lady of Dolours; and on Saturday he totally abstained from food. He was accustomed to rise at midnight to meditate on her sorrows. The Blessed Virgin knew how to reward him; appearing to him while yet young, she bade him enter the Order of her servants, which injunction he obeyed. Towards the close of his life she showed him two crowns—one of rubies, in recompense for his life-long compassion for her griefs; the other of pearls, in reward of the purity he had consecrated under her patronage. Lastly, she appeared to him at death. The Blessed Joachim then begged the favour of dying on the same day as our Lord. "Prepare, then," Mary said to him, "for to-morrow, Friday, you shall have your wish, and die suddenly; to-morrow you shall be with me in Paradise." In effect, the next day, as the Passion according to St. John was being sung in the Church, when they came to the words—" There stood by the Cross of Jesus His Mother," Joachim fainted away ; and at this other passage—" And bowing His Head, He gave up the ghost," he breathed his last, and the church was filled with great light and a very sweet perfume.

TWENTY-SEVENTH DAY.

THE CLIENT OF MARY SHOULD BE DEVOTED TO THE SALVATION OF SOULS.

"Let your voice," the voice which asks for the life of my erring children, "sound in my ears" (Cant. ii. 14.)

IF such as we are, just and sinners, we can all boast of the glorious title of children of Mary, if it be true that she is our Mother, that she loves us a thousand times more than any mother can love her child, alas! how rent and torn must our Mother's Heart be! How many rebellious and ungrateful children does she count! How many does she behold daily perish before her eyes! What is the grief of a mother from whose embrace death has snatched a beloved child; how bitter seems to her all the joys and consolations of the world, now that her little one is no longer visible! Such, and incomparably more inexpressible still, is the pain of Mary's Heart when she beholds children that cost her so dear suspended over the abyss of perdition, on the point of being engulfed therein for ever. This sight was for her, during her life, a continued martyrdom, as she disclosed to one of her friends, and one capable of causing her death at each instant, had not God by His power preserved her. Oh! how ardently she besought her Divine Son to restore to her those children of her sorrow. What tears accompanied her supplications! How willingly would she have undergone a thousand deaths for each one of them!

Can we, then, we whom the Lord hath regarded

in His mercy, we who are so happy as to comprehend, to share in the anguish of our Mother, can we believe we really love her, and not cast ourselves at the feet of the divine justice to obtain the revocation of that decree impending over the heads of our brethren, to wrest from the enemy souls so dearly loved by our Mother? Through her exertions, doubtless, some are restored to life; but alas! "What are these among so many?"— *Sed quid sunt inter tantos?** The Holy Ghost compares the souls that profit by the Redemption to the few olives that remain after the gathering, to the grapes left behind when the vintage is ended.† Poor souls! St. Mary Magdalen de Pazzi saw them fall into hell, like to flakes of a heavy snowstorm in winter! Mary, to whom we are indebted for all, expects that we will come to her aid, in rescuing them from so dire a calamity; not that she wants either the ability or desire to succour them, but she requires to be besought to this effect, and such is the proof of love she demands from us.

All we, children of Mary, whether we have known her, loved her from infancy, whether she has withdrawn us from death to the admirable light amidst which her children walk, let us unite to attract a great number of souls in our track; let us never cease with uplifted hands to implore Heaven in behalf of our brethren engaged in the battle of life, and on the point of succumbing to the efforts of their enemies; let us not remain insensible to their perils, their disasters, the mortal wounds with which they are covered; let us parry the thrusts aimed at them, let us snatch them from

* St. John vi. 9.   † Isaias xxiv. 13.

eternal perdition; let us cry out with the Church —"Save, O Mother, save your people, your children, bless your inheritance, but bless them with that omnipotent benediction which makes the elect, the Saints"—*Salvum fac populum tuum, et benedic hæreditati tuæ.*

Let us unite in heart and affections with the Archconfraternity of the Sacred Heart of Mary, which has so wonderfully discovered the way to that Heart which forgets self to think of perishing souls. Let us pray, and let us be assured of the success of our prayers. In effect, in all my other petitions I may be mistaken; if I solicit health, life for myself or others, these gifts might be, perchance, the greatest misfortunes; but when, touched by the danger incurred by my brethren, I implore Mary to grant me their souls, when I repeat to her a thousand times a day, "Give me souls"—*Da mihi animas;* then it is I may pray with confidence, with importunity. This gift that I solicit, the Blood of Jesus, the most ardent desire of Mary's Heart, sustains me in asking it. Far from my prayer being importunate to the Mother of Mercy, she longs for it impatiently; she is not wearied with its repetition, and seems to say to me in her turn—"Ah! let your voice, that voice that supplicates life for my erring children, sound again and again in my ears—*Sonet vox tua in auribus meis.** Pray, beseech, again and again, be never wearied, I can accomplish more than you can even hope for."

A great servant of God, Sister Seraphina of Capria, having besought the Blessed Virgin, during the novena of her Assumption, to grant her the

---

* Cant. ii. 14.

conversion of a thousand sinners, afterwards feared having asked too much. Mary, chiding her for this vain fear, said—" Do you believe, then, that I have not sufficient credit with my Son to obtain the conversion of a thousand sinners? I grant them to you at once."

But would it be forgetting our own interests thus to employ all our prayers and good works for the salvation of souls? Far from it, it is to fulfil the greatest, the first of the commandments, that in which all others are comprised; it is to love God with the most perfect love, to love the neighbour as much and more than self, after the example of Jesus and Mary; it is to love Him even as these divine models have loved us. "This is My commandment, that you love one another as I have loved you."

Oh! how powerful over Mary's heart in favour of self is the soul that has saved even one of her children from eternal perdition! Could this compassionate Mother deny her anything during the days of her pilgrimage! And when her hour of death has arrived, how easy will she contrive to render that final journey to her! How tenderly will she say to her, in welcoming her to Heaven, " Arise, my beloved—*Surge amica mea;* you sympathized with me in my heaviest tribulations, you won back to me souls redeemed with the precious Blood of my Son; come to be crowned at the hands of your Mother—*Veni coronaberis.* Enter into the joy, the merits of these poor souls, enter into the joy of your Mother, and that of my Divine Son Himself, 'enter into the joy of thy Lord'— *Intra in gaudium Domini tui.*"

Practice.—*To pray for sinners* is before God one of the most precious spiritual works of mercy;

it is to cooperate, as far as lies in us, in the work of the redemption, to practise that great charity that covereth a multitude of sins—*Charitas operit multitudinem peccatorum.** Therefore let no day pass without recommending to Jesus and Mary these souls so dearly purchased by them. Should you be a member of the Archconfraternity of the Immaculate Heart of Mary, which is devoted to this work, not only be faithful to the "Hail Mary" prescribed, but in order to enter into the true spirit of this Association, act so that, at least in intention, all your good works may be directed to this sublime end—"The greater glory of God through Mary, and the salvation of souls."

Aspiration.—O Mary! reserve for others the riches of this world; all *I* desire, all I ask of you, is souls—*Da mihi animas, cætera tolle tibi.*†

Example.

Mr. D——, who had formerly served in the navy, was a frank and loyal man; but there his religion ended. He held Priests in abhorrence, had received none but the first of the Sacraments, and Matrimony without confession. He was in the fiftieth year of his age. An invalid for a long period, his illness assumed a serious aspect in the beginning of the year 1834, and he was obliged to keep his bed. In a short time the physicians declared his case hopeless. His daughter, educated at a convent in Paris, had made her first Communion some months before; and her father, already attacked by the chest disease which finally carried him off, was at that time a great source of

---

* 1 St. Peter iv. 8.   † Gen. xiv. 21.

solicitude. She was often found bathed in tears, and when interrogated as to the cause of her grief, she would reply—" Papa is so ill, and he will die without Sacraments." She had, so to speak, solicited but one favour on the day of first Communion—*the conversion of her father*, and her companions had joined their supplications to hers, for the same intention. These pious children persevered for eight months, with Leonie, in soliciting the same favour.

Not till the last hour was this happy elect one to be called by God. Mary, Refuge of Sinners, was for him the channel of grace. A relative of the sick man, a Nun, attempted to write to him, and although she did not approach the main point, Mr. D——, fearing something more serious, flings the letter aside, saying, "My cousin would have me confess and communicate; but I have no faith in these formalities—they are mere priestcraft; besides, I have neither killed nor stolen. I thank God, I am an honourable man, and I have the fullest confidence in the divine mercy." Sister B——, sent by his relative to visit him, replied, that if he consented to see a Priest, this latter would soon prove to him that to ensure salvation it required more than to be an honest man. "Above all, bring none of these folk about me," said he, with vivacity, "I will positively not see them."

Every second day Sister B—— visited her patient, with no greater success. It then became evident that they should look to God alone. Accordingly, they began a novena of *Memorares*, and caused a miraculous medal to be presented to the sick man, with a request that he would wear it for fifteen days, and then restore it; it would then be, his cousin said, a remembrance of him, which she would be happy to preserve. "Oh!" said he, "I am not to be duped by this trick. After all," he added, smilingly, "it will feel like two *sous* in my pocket. But stay, to show you that I am not prejudiced, I will wear it on my neck." The effect of the powerful intercession of the Mother of Mercy was so prompt, that by the morrow our patient had altered both language and sentiments. "I know not how it is," he said, "but I would not be sorry if you brought me a Priest; I would willingly see him." However, they deemed it advisable not to be in a hurry. The day following, not only was he in the same frame of mind, but was even extremely disturbed that his request had not yet been complied with. "Do call in Mr. C——," he asked; "I am impatient to see him. I am sensible I have no faith; but I desire nothing so much as to possess it. Pray get others to pray that I may believe. Confession," he continued, "is not the main point;" so had this faith he had so heartily invoked already grown in his heart; "it is absolution. What if I profaned the Sacrament, if I made a sacrilegious Communion?" "Then your faith is greater than you think." "No, it is only I desire to have it; pray, for I wish to perform the act in a Christian manner."

In effect Mr. C—— came, and began by discussing with him those points of religion that most perplexed him—the mysteries, the scandal given by bad Christians, &c. &c. He fully satisfied him. "I am enchanted," he said to Sister B——, when she came to see him; "Mr. C—— told me he did not understand the mysteries better than myself, and that I was not obliged to comprehend them in order to be saved. Ah! how I regret," he added, "not to have known religion sooner. I fancied it a monster, and now I see it produces only consolations."

A still more reassuring feature in this conversion was, that the sufferer, like all consumptive patients, had no idea of death; nay, promised himself a speedy recovery. "I am prepared," he often said, "to fulfil whatever religion prescribes. I have made Mr. C—— a disclosure of my entire life, but this is not sufficient." In effect, he had not yet made his confession. God permitting him a few days after this to experience a violent crisis, during which his death was feared, Mr. C—— was sent for in haste. He heard his confession, and gave him absolution. "My good Father," said the patient, when all was concluded, "when you have a few moments to lose, come, spend them with this poor sinner." Next day, the Holy Oils were administered to him, also the Viaticum, which was his first Communion. During the interval, he had asked his daughter, a girl of twelve, to recite with him appropriate acts. Seeing the credence table, whereon the Blessed Sacrament was to be laid, he said, "Bring Leonie's statue of the Blessed Virgin, and place it here." It was to Mary he owed his happiness, and so would have her preside at the ceremony. Moreover, as he had often discussed religious points with a good Christian lady, a relative of his, he wished, in reparation of the scandal he might have given her, to make her a witness of his sincere conversion, and had her invited to be present on the day he was administered. He remained in profound recollection until the arrival of Mr. C——. After the short exhortation which was addressed to him, he offered his hands himself to be anointed, with so penetrated, so reverent an air, it moved all present to tears. He then received Holy Communion.

When Sister B—— and Mr. C—— were taking leave, he said, "I cannot find words to express the happiness I feel, and my heartfelt gratitude for all your cares. Mr. C—— declared that never in the whole course of his ministry had he witnessed so sincere a return on a death-bed, nor had he ever experienced so much consolation in the administration of the last Sacraments.

Our patient had been only in time in his measures, for next day he felt much worse, and vomited blood. His friends continued their visits, and he invariably begged for prayers, adding, "Oh, you do not know what a great sinner I am." Whenever the acts of faith, hope, and charity, or any other short prayer was suggested to him, although he could hardly turn in the bed, he sat up, to recite them more respectfully. He had received the last Sacraments in the afternoon of Thursday, 5th February, Feast of the Japonian Martyrs, and on the following Sunday, at five o'clock in the morning, he expired, calmly, without agony, God, by a last effect of His mercy, sparing him the terrors usually attendant on the last passage, and the final combat against the enemy of salvation. Happy, a thousand times happy, for that, being called only at the last hour through the mediation of Mary, the hope of the forlorn, he merited to receive the reward with those who had borne "the burden of the day and the heats."

TWENTY-EIGHTH DAY.

THE TRUE CHILD OF MARY SHOULD IMITATE HER VIRTUES.

"To imitate what we revere, this is true devotion" (St. Augustine).

"BE ye, therefore, followers of God, as most dear children."* The imitation of your Mother's virtues is the mark by which you will be recognized as her beloved children: such is the obligation incumbent on you, by your very title of child of Mary; endeavour to fulfil it.

But what are the virtues Mary practised? To what perfection did she attain in each? This is not given to human intellect to fathom. Let it suffice for us to know that she alone among pure creatures has entirely fulfilled these words of her Divine Son. "Be you therefore perfect, as also your Heavenly Father is perfect."†

Among the many virtues that shone conspicuously in Mary, three there are which it gives her special satisfaction to reign in the hearts of her children—*purity, humility*, and *obedience*.

1. *Purity.*—Purity of body, of mind, and heart, it is you that have attracted the Divine Word into the womb of Mary. Whoever understands you, understands the highest perfection, nay, has attained it. Purity of heart and intention, that continual turning of the soul to God, with a habitual forgetfulness of self, is that so much sought for philosopher's stone, which converts the least of our actions into gold for eternity. It is this look of the Spouse

* Ephes. v. 1. † St. Matt. v. 48.

which wounds, transpierces the Heart of God, and effects the conquest of It; it is the first, the last, the most powerful spring in spiritual life, one which may not be left an instant idle, under penalty of retrograding in the ways of God.

2. *Humility*, the guardian, the safeguard of all virtues. What a flood of light did it not pour on Mary! For weak, helpless creatures like us to confess we are nothing—what more natural? But it is from the most prodigious elevation God Himself could devise for honouring human nature, that Mary, Mother of God, praises the Lord, because "He hath regarded the humility of His handmaid." Whence proceeds such a fund of abasement in this divine Mother? It is that she sees by the light of Heaven, that a mere creature before God is nothing, absolutely nothing, even though Mother of God. What, then, are we? O humility! what a sway you exercise over the Heart of the Most High. Speak, souls that seek after God, when did you find Him? when had you a sensible perception of the presence of His grace? when did He incline towards you with greater condescension? It was when He took care to humble you, made you feel your own weakness, your offences, your misery, your incapacity for good; it was when you humbled yourself, acknowledged your own vileness in His sight—*Et anima mea facta est vilis;* when you gladly embraced, or, at least, supported with patience, humiliation; for God places His privileged gifts only in humble souls, because only such honour Him; all others reserving to themselves the *glory*, that substance, that marrow of His gifts which God has jealously reserved for Himself.

3. *Obedience.*—Here we are not to understand it

as vowed by certain privileged souls, but that obedience to God, that *submission* of mind and heart *to His will*, which ought to be the virtue of all Christians. This virtue will elevate your soul proportionally to its docility, its subjection to God. You will no longer be controlled by men, or events; in every circumstance you will see God, His providence, with a feeling of submission and joy. " It is the Lord"—*Dominus est.* It is He Who visits me in these contradictions, He who ordains these trials. It is His hand presents me this cross—the same cross He has borne for my love. " Shall not my soul be subject to God?"*

What a fund of rest and peace of mind is submission to the divine will, amidst the afflictions that beset this life! Children of Mary, to reanimate your courage in your efforts for the acquisition of this virtue, recall at the price of what sacrifices your divine Mother exercised it.

Practice.—" My little children," Mary seems to say by the mouth of the Beloved Disciple, "*love me not in word only, but in deed and in truth.*" That is to say, be not content to offer me the homage of your prayers, but endeavour, above all, to copy my virtues; for the Kingdom of Heaven is the reward of those that do violence; none but the generous-hearted and resolute bear it away. Be therefore careful to join to prayer, struggle and action. " He that doth these things, shall not be moved for ever"—*Qui facit hæc non movebitur in æternum.*

Aspiration.—Grant, O Mary, that I may imitate you, in order to prove my love!

* Psalm lx. 1.

Example.

St. Louis, the pride and model of French monarchs, owed his birth to the protection of Mary and the Devotion of the holy Rosary. The pious Queen Blanche of Castile ardently desired to give an heir to the throne according to God's own Heart. St. Dominic, who was then living, counselled her to have recourse to the Blessed Virgin and the holy Rosary, to recite it frequently, and to engage such of her subjects as were known to her for their piety to pay in her name the same homage to our Blessed Lady, giving her to hope that through the patronage of the Mother of Mercy she should obtain the desired blessing. Blanche followed this counsel with as much fidelity as success. The virtue of the holy Rosary, and the piety of the Princess, produced the desired effect. She became mother of a son, in whose person sanctity itself was enthroned, who hallowed his crown by every Christian virtue, illustrated his life by the most heroic actions; in a word, who carried his baptismal robe unsullied to the tomb, enriched with all the merits that constitute Saints, and very eminent Saints. So tender and lively was his devotion to the Mother of God, and such the love he entertained for her humility, that, to honour and imitate it, he had assembled every Saturday within his palace, even in his own apartment, a crowd of poor persons. There, after the example of his Saviour, he washed their feet in a basin, and wiping them with his royal hands, kissed them with a respect which clearly showed he recognized in them the members of Jesus Christ. After that, to join charity to humility, he made them dine, himself waiting upon them at table, esteeming himself happier a thousand times in thus rendering glory to Jesus and Mary, than in receiving the homage of his whole Court.

Finally, he terminated so edifying a ceremony, by distributing to each a rich alms, likewise in honour of the Queen of Heaven and earth. It had been his desire to die on a Saturday, as though to crown, by the homage of his last sigh, all the honours he had each week of his life paid to Mary on that day. His wish was granted, Mary desiring that this day, devoted to her, should likewise be for her faithful servant that of his entrance into eternal glory.

* Psalm xvi. 5.

TWENTY-NINTH DAY.

FIDELITY TO OUR DEVOTIONAL EXERCISES TO MARY.

"Do little if you will in Mary's honour, but be constant" (Blessed Berchmans).

IN the *Revelations of St. Bridget,* Mary is styled "Harbinger of the Sun"—*Sidus vadens ante solem,* which gives to understand that when a soul begins to feel devotion to the Blessed Virgin, it is a certain sign that God will speedily come to enrich her with His graces.

"Mary, Mother of my God," used St. John Damascene to say, "if I confide in you, my salvation is assured; under your protection I have nothing to fear, for devotion to you is a powerful weapon, which God places in the hands of those He desires to save." Christian soul, if you discover in yourself a true sentiment of affection and reverence for the Queen of Heaven, bless the Lord a thousand times, but guard sedulously this pledge of salvation; ask Mary herself to preserve it to you, and neglect nothing to keep so precious a treasure. For we carry this grace in frail vessels; it may be weakened, we may render ourselves unworthy of it. How many souls now groaning in the eternal abyss have loved Mary, served her, been objects of her special favour! How, then, came these brilliant stars to fall from the height to which their ardent devotion to Mary had raised them? Alas! they tired of this way of salvation, they abandoned first one exercise, then another; little infidelities led on to great; and they ran in the path of iniquity even more swiftly than they had run in that of justice. They had begun well, they ended badly, therefore their lot is in the pool of fire and brimstone.

What is to be done to escape a like misfortune? To determine what practises of devotion you shall prescribe for yourselves in honour of Mary, and be inviolably faithful to them in every state and vicissitude of spirit: in fervour and aridity, in consolation and desolation, in the turmoil of business, and the calm of repose and solitude; should you even fall into sin, into disorder, lay not aside your invincible arms—the love, the invocation of Mary; persist but the more resolutely in their exercise, not for a month, for a certain time, on special Feasts, but every day of your life—you will thus baffle all the wiles of your enemy.

It is related of Blessed John Berchmans that, being interrogated by his Brethren on his death-bed on the practices of devotion by which they could best please Mary and obtain her protection, he replied, "The least things, provided you be constant"—*Minimum, sed constans*. Follow this counsel, whose practice has saved so many souls; do but little if you will, but let nothing prevail on you to omit what you have once imposed. Some in a moment of fervour go beyond the bounds of discretion; then, when grace is withdrawn, they abandon even the most ordinary practices. As to you, be convinced that love is proved more by an abiding fidelity, than by passing transports of fervour. Father Claude de la Columbière regulated each retreat what he would perform for the glory of Mary, and so became annually renovated in his devotion to the Mother of God. Do the same every year during the month of May; examine at the feet of Mary what has been your fidelity in her service; ask pardon of your Mother, repair your want of ardour in praising her during the year which has just elapsed, and devoting yourself anew to her love, say in the words of the royal Prophet, "Now I will begin"—*Nunc cœpi.* Yes, O Mary! now, from this day, I will strive to become one of your most zealous servants; now I will begin to love you. Alas! hitherto I was not in earnest in my attempts, or if I did put my hand to the task, ere long, looking back, I yielded to tepidity and negligence. O Mary! O my Mother! confirm the change you have wrought in me—*Confirma hoc, . . . quod operatus es.* Let devotion to you—the devotion of the elect—take so deep root in me, that it may never be effaced.* Grant me this favour, O Mary! for the glory of Him Who loved me and delivered Himself for me.

Practice.—Among the numerous exercises in Mary's honour, at your selection, there are some you should be faithful to observe.

1. *Daily.*—Recitation of the *Memorare*, the Beads, the Litany, or some other prayer at your choice.

2. *Weekly.*—On Saturday, the day consecrated to her, you may propose to honour Mary by some mortification, alms, prayer, or special visit to one of her statues, chapels, &c.

3. *Monthly.*—To assist at Mass on the first Saturday, really or in spirit; communicate thereat, whether spiritually or sacramentally; to visit the sick, the poor; to instruct the ignorant in her honour, &c.

* Ecclus. xxiv.

4. *Yearly.*—To make the month of May with renewed fervour.

It would be advisable to determine which you will adopt, even to arrange the time of day for performing them, that so indecision may not furnish a pretext for their omission.

Aspiration.—Mary, I have sworn, and am determined to keep the law of your love; be yourself my security, for without you I can do nothing!

Example.

The venerable Thomas à Kempis evinced from childhood quite a special devotion to the Blessed Virgin. He had imposed on himself a daily tribute of praise in her honour, which he was exact to fulfil. Nevertheless, his devotion cooled insensibly; he omitted his accustomed exercises, one day, two days, an entire week, and finally discontinued them altogether. It was then that a mysterious dream made him sensible of the gravity of his fault. He appeared to be in the class-room with his fellow-students, listening attentively to the lecture. He thought he saw the Queen of Heaven descend upon clouds, her countenance radiant, her garments of dazzling white. She appeared to make the round of the apartment, stopping beside each Religious engaged in the instruction of youth, speak to them kindly, and giving them the sweetest tokens of her maternal affection. Thomas seeing this, awaited with the most lively impatience the approach of the Holy Virgin; he cast on her looks that bespoke the ardour of his desires. He said to himself--"I confess that I am undeserving of these testimonies of affection from the Mother of God; I hope, however, I hope." He hoped but he was much deceived in his expectation! Mary presented herself before him, appeared to regard him with a severe eye; and, far from giving him marks of tenderness, she reproached him for his culpable negligence, his base docility to the suggestions of the devil. "Where," she said, are the prayers so fervent, those Rosaries and Offices recited with so tender devotion? And yet you presume to expect testimonies of my love? Go! Depart from me! You are unworthy of my tenderness, seeing that you neglect to offer exercises so easy to her whom heretofore you loved." At these words she vanished, leaving him in consternation. Awaking from sleep, he examined his conscience, humbly acknowledged his fault, and promised to amend. He resumed his pious exercises with so great fervour and constancy, that never till his dying hour did he omit them for a single day. O blessed rebuke! it reinstated in the right path a soul that had just begun to withdraw therefrom, and stopped him perhaps on the brink of the precipice.*

* *Mois de Marie.* By Père Bussi.

THIRTIETH DAY.

OF THE ZEAL THAT MARY EXPECTS FROM HER CHILDREN IN MAKING HER KNOWN AND LOVED.

May zeal for thy glory consume me, O Mary!

CHILDREN of Mary, it suffices not that your hearts expand with devotion to your Mother; that remembrance of her absorbs all the faculties of your soul; that you adhere to her by bonds of tenderest love: you must moreover enkindle this delightful fire in all hearts. In Mary you have found the treasure of eternal life; hoard it not up for yourself alone. Let your zeal for your Mother's honour be inflamed therefore; arise together, and proclaim everywhere that she is holy, all powerful, blessed; inspire all hearts with the same love that burns in your own. Yours will not be a difficult task, for so sweet, so natural, so legitimate is this devotion, that even he who seems to have forgotten his God, would not venture to admit he had forgotten Mary, his Mother. There are few hearts so opposed to their own interests as to cast aside this last means of salvation; few, at least, who refuse at the solicitation of a parent, or zealous friend, to devote themselves to Mary by some daily prayers, the wearing of a medal of the Holy Virgin. And this once obtained, we all know how Mary finds the secret of entering hearts the most indifferent, the most rebellious, and making herself the Mistress of them. These appear very feeble expedients for bringing about so great a result; but it is precisely because they seem so remote from the end, that they are less suspected. It is because they are so weak that God is pleased to triumph by them over rebellious wills, that man may learn that all his prudence and cunning are as nought in the conversion of souls. Children of Mary, humble disciples of the humblest of Virgins, bless her then, for that she has chosen you to initiate you into these secrets, which God conceals from the wise and prudent. Assume your arms, the medal of Mary, prayer to Mary; it is by these signs you will conquer; it is by these signs you will make Mary known, by which she will obtain access to hearts.

Tell the just to increase, let him become on fire with this love, which, if not daily fed and increased, slackens and becomes finally extinguished. Stir up the tepid, by repeating to them, that he who is faithless, negligent in minor practices in honour of Mary, ends by forsaking her service and becoming lost. But if you desire to make prompt and durable conquests, begin your apostolate by childhood; make Mary known to those innocent hearts so suited to comprehend and love her.

Long tried experience proves that impressions received in youth grow with the soul, and outlive all the storms of passion. You may afterwards try your strength in better contested victories; betake yourself to the lost sheep of the house of Israel, make Mary known to those who are tired out in the way of iniquity, who seek in vain for satisfaction in enjoyments that have so often deceived them already: in this way of salvation, the delights of which they were far from suspecting, they shall acquire new heart and soul.

Children of Mary, happy are you to have been chosen to announce the name, the glory, the power of your Mother! You know the reward for your zeal. Oftentimes, to stimulate you, has she whispered to your heart—"Courage, good and faithful servant, I am with you in the toils, the tribulations you endure for my name; and a day will come when eternal glory, a seat nearer your Mother's throne, will be the reward of those praises rendered by yourself and those you shall have procured her, by teaching others to know and love her."

Practice.—Neglect nothing to induce all over whom you have influence to cherish a tender and solid devotion to Mary. The distribution of books which treat of her, the upholding the practices of piety authorized by the Church in her honour; such are the means which Mary's love suggests for propagating devotion to her. Be faithful in employing them, but be not less assiduous in exciting yourself to this love, lest, after having taught it to others, you should remain stationary yourself in this way of salvation, in which not to advance is to recede.

Aspiration.—May the name of Mary be known, praised, blessed, and glorified for ever.

Example.

Blessed Alphonsus Rodriguez made it his duty to speak of spiritual matters to all with whom he held intercourse, recommending especially the recital of the Rosary, and enlarging on the inestimable advantage derived from the frequent use of the Sacraments of Penance and the Holy Eucharist. Devotion to Mary was the theme on which he usually conversed with seculars, and he skilfully turned this noble subject to account, to induce sinners to apply confidently to her who is their refuge, at the same time that he made them sensible that external practices avail not to Mary's honour, if her maternal Heart is rent by outrages against her Divine Son. The children who frequented the College were not less sharers in the charity of this good Brother. He taught them the Christian doctrine, inspired them with a tender affection for the Queen of Virgins, and suggested to them little practices of piety, proportioned to their years and necessities.

In fine, he applied himself with equal zeal in behalf of the poor who came to seek relief at the College gates, mingling with his instructions apposite reflections and most pathetic exhortations.

Another skilful means made use of by this servant, to contribute as far as lay in his power to the salvation of his neighbour, was fervently to intreat God for the success of preachers and other evangelical labourers. He earnestly besought His Divine Majesty to confer on His ministers those virtues that constitute Apostles, and to render them powerful in word and work. Nor did Alphonsus neglect, when a fitting opportunity occurred, to insinuate to the Religious of the house who were engaged in the holy ministry, that the most effectual means for sanctifying others was to labour at their own perfection.

THIRTY-FIRST DAY.

CONSECRATION TO MARY.

"It is impossible for any one on whom you look to perish, O Mary!"
(St. Anselm).

BEHOLD, then, this month of grace and benediction come to a conclusion! Do the effects correspond with the resolution so generously formed at its commencement, of passing it in fervour? Thank Mary, your fidelity is a gift of her love. Have you to accuse yourself of tepidity? Let your confusion surpass in some measure your negligence; Mary will not despise a contrite and humble heart. With Jesus and Mary good days have no end. If we desire it, the end of this month will be the beginning of a life of love and devotedness to this divine Mother, and though you cease to assemble daily at her feet, you will erect an altar in your heart whereon you will offer her the incense of prayer and praise every day of your life.

But it may be that, feeling your own weakness so frequently experienced, you say, in the bitterness of your soul—"Already many times have I begun—promised Mary to love her, to pray to her, to imitate her, and sad experience has convinced me of the fruitlessness of my promises, my repentance. I deceive God, or rather, I deceive myself." Do you desire to secure your fidelity, take Mary as a guarantee; consecrate to her to-day irrevocably all you are, retain nothing for yourself, make her a generous surrender of your entire being; adopt the salutary custom of renewing every morning this act of consecration in a few words, and you will see that what she keeps is well kept, if her inheritance is not with the Saints, if they with whom she journeys can ever weary in the way of her love.

Act of Consecration to the Blessed Virgin.

O Mary, my Mother, I know that those who hope in you are never confounded. The bitter waters of tribulation may pass over their head, yet are they not engulfed therein; they may dwell amid the devouring flames of the Babylonian furnace, but are not consumed; alone they may be without strength or virtue, but no sooner do they become devoted to you than their energies are transformed, you indue them with your own strength, and they soar like eagles, never wearying in the paths of salvation. Penetrated with the sentiment of my own misery and inconstancy, I lift my eyes to you, O Mary! To you do I stretch out my hands, in your powerful protection put my trust; only espouse my cause and I shall no longer have to blush at my weakness, nor shall my enemies deride the fruitlessness of my efforts. O my Mother, I desire that, in defending my soul, you may henceforth be defending your own property, your own inheritance. Therefore I pray you to accept the entire, irrevocable consecration I make you of my whole being for time and eternity. I consecrate to your maternal and immaculate Heart my body, heart, soul, and mind, my life here and hereafter. I desire that henceforth there may be nothing in me which is not immolated to your praise.

O Mary! may your name be the first to rise to my lips in temptation; may love and remembrance of you be my solace in pain and suffering; may they be to me a substitute for all the vain joys of this world. For you let me labour, for you suffer; let nothing be agreeable to me without you, O Mary! May each instant of my life be a reiterated appeal to your protection, and a protestation of the love with which I fain would burn for you. May I live and die in your arms, and rejoice for ever with you for the glory to which you are elevated. O Mary! Daughter of the Father, Mother of the Son, Spouse of the Holy Ghost, and yet no less my Mother.

Aspiration.—My heart is no longer mine, my heart is Mary's.

Practice.—It seems as though we were looking forward to some future moment, in which we shall decidedly and seriously labour at the affair of our salvation, and yet this moment ever recedes, life glides on, and we remain empty-handed. Nevertheless, sanctity is within our grasp; it consists not in things uncommon, great, or difficult, but in the *perfection of our ordinary actions.* What marvels did our Lord effect during the thirty years of His hidden life, or the Blessed Virgin during a long career of more than seventy years? Nothing that does not come within the scope of our habitual occupations, and also nothing which was not enhanced, deified, by the intention, by the perfection accompanying each action. Let us, then, endeavour to perform even our most indifferent actions with all the application of which God has rendered us capable. This is the practical way to true and solid sanctity.

Example.

St. Alphonsus Ligouri was indebted to his pious mother for that tender devotion to the Blessed Virgin which was his characteristic. While yet a child, he one day broke away suddenly from his playmates, who were hotly disputing among themselves. Long after they discovered him in a remote spot, prostrate before a little picture of Mary, which he had fastened to a laurel tree, and so absorbed was he that the noise of their approach did not in the least disturb his holy recollection. Moreover, this pious child suffered no day to pass without going to pray to Mary, whether in a church or at the foot of an altar dedicated to her. Already he fasted on bread and water every Saturday in her honour, and this custom he observed during his whole life, till forbidden by his confessor in his declining years. He had shone for some time at the Bar, when an interior voice whispered with irresistible force—"What business have you in the world?" "Lord, here I am; what will you have me to do?" was his reply. And entering into an adjoining church, that of the Redemption of Captives, he prostrated himself before the Blessed Sacrament, conjuring our Lord to accept the sacrifice which he made of his entire being. Then, taking off his sword, he hung it at the altar of our Lady of Mercy, as an authentic pledge of his inviolable consecration to the divine will. This happy day he styled that of his conversion, and whenever he came to Naples he failed not to visit the statue of Mary which had received his vow of fidelity.

In the sequel, he wished all his penitents to have a picture of Mary in their chamber, near the bed.

He recommended them his own favourite practice, that of fasting on Saturdays and the eves of her principal Festivals. He, moreover, desired they should prepare for them by a novena, as he did.

He was most exact in saying the beads daily, and in consecrating every hour by the recital of the "Hail Mary." Whenever the clock struck he was seen to break off abruptly in the middle of a conversation to comply with this pious custom, no matter by whom surrounded. To such as expressed surprise at this he replied—"One 'Hail Mary' is a treasure surpassing that of the whole world." Nor did he ever omit the *Angelus*, kneeling down at the first sound of the bell, were he even in the public streets; if he happened to be at table he left off eating and fell on his knees. The fervour with which he acquitted himself of these little practices, which custom frequently renders mechanical, was truly edifying; it often happened that he was wrapt in ecstasy while reciting the *Angelus*.

To honour Mary's sufferings during the Passion was a favourite devotion of Alphonsus. He frequently invoked her in his sermons, inviting sinners to solicit through her intercession the pardon of their crimes. To this end he had a statue of our Lady of Dolours placed beside the pulpit during his missions.

Before he became Bishop he preached every Saturday on the greatness of Mary in the church of his Congregation. He did the same in his Cathedral, or some other church in his place of residence, when not out of his diocese. He had ordered this practice to be observed in all the Houses of his Institute. He deemed his disciples bound in gratitude to render this homage to the Queen of Heaven. He never wearied in extolling the power of Mary and the efficacy of her intercession, and laboured like St. Bernard to enforce this maxim, authorized by the other Fathers—that "no true servant of Mary can perish." He gave to all who visited him a picture of the Blessed Virgin, and, his soul expanding, found affectionate words in which he exhorted them to vow a tender love to her, and to have entire confidence in her protection. "In all your necessities," used he to say, "betake yourselves to her, place your hope in her alone."

Mary did not suffer herself to be vanquished in love by her faithful servant, and historians relate, among other favours conferred on him, the following—"Preaching a novena at Foggia in honour of the miraculous image venerated there, he one day lingered in the church after the crowd had dispersed, through devotion. Happening to cast his eyes on the holy image he fell into an ecstasy, which lasted an hour. The picture appeared as though living, and of ravishing beauty. She bowed to her servant, and regarded him with an expression of incomparable tenderness. Alphonsus remained there the whole time motionless, his eyes fixed on Mary. When the vision ceased he intoned the *Ave Maris Stella*, in which he was joined by all present. Another time, while he was preaching at St. George's on the greatness of Mary, and exhorting his hearers to confidence, the people thought he was an Angel rather than a man. Presently they beheld a wondrous ray of light issue from the person of Mary; it traversed the whole church, and settled on the face of Alphonsus. At the same time the latter, falling into a rapture, was raised several feet from the ground. At this sight the congregation shouted with wonder and delight, so that their cries were heard at a great distance. More than four thousand persons were witnesses of this miracle.*

The works, sermons, and prayers composed by St. Ligouri, the *Visits to the Blessed Virgin*, which follow each visit to the Blessed Sacrament, attest his singular devotion to the Mother of God. Above all, his book entitled the *Glories of Mary* is a striking testimony of his zeal and devotedness to his potent Protectress.

* Rohrbacher.

Visits to the Blessed Sacrament during the Month of May.

FIRST VISIT.

MYSTERY OF FAITH—"MYSTERIUM FIDEI."

Credo, Domine, adjuva incredulitatem meam—"*I do believe, Lord, help my unbelief*" (St. Mark ix. 23).

"MY GOD," as the great Bossuet used to say, "that I may have no difficulty in yielding my understanding to you, I begin by submitting it; not only concerning all the works of nature, but more than all the rest, concerning myself." All is mystery around me, in me; how much greater reason for mystery in religion! But the mystery of mysteries is Your abasement, Your annihilation, in the Eucharist. My senses, my reason, there lose themselves. My senses behold nothing real; sight, taste, touch, contradict my belief. *Visus, gustus, tactus in te fallitur.* Faith alone, the word of God, Who said, "This is My Body, this is My Blood," must be confidently relied on. My blind reason is here still more confounded than my senses. Why, how, for what purpose, thus reverse all the laws of nature? God has spoken, I believe. A God-Man, what a prodigy already! but a God-Man under the appearance of bread! Prostrate and suppliant I adore You, O Divinity doubly concealed! Yes, under those sacred species my faith discovers you. On the Cross your Godhead alone was veiled, here even your Humanity disappears from my eyes. Yet do I confess and believe both; I ask but one grace, with the penitent thief—Lord, my God, *remember me*, here in this tabernacle, all the days of my life, remember me in Your kingdom, that I may merit there to contemplate, there to love your Divinity and Humanity for ever, after having adored them here in the darkness of faith.

O Mary, blessed because you have believed. I believe, help my unbelief—*Credo, adjuva incredulitatem meam.*

SECOND VISIT.

MYSTERY OF HOPE.

In Te Domine speravi, non confundar in aeternum—"*In Thee, O Lord, have I hoped, let me never be confounded.*"

How often does hope, our soul's chief support here below, seem to forsake us, O Lord my God! Life is so sad, so painful, its dangers so multiplied, great, and continued, our weakness such, that our heart frequently fails us in the way. There are situations so grievous, so desperate, that we seem ready to allow ourselves to be borne away by the current, not caring to prolong a fruitless struggle; strength, courage, everything fails us at once. Events, mankind, still more ourselves, all seem to cast me into an abyss of indifference and despair. But, my dear Lord, should all fade around me, within me, when I remember You, abiding with me, so constant in bearing me company in this Sacrament, I seem to return to life. No, all is not lost for me, for this miserable world, since You have deigned to dwell in the midst of us, within us, till the end of time. My fellow-creatures and I are, therefore, something great, noble, dignified, that a God should occupy Himself thus with us, descend daily from Heaven into our prison—*Descenditque cum illo in foveam.* If such be His assiduity towards His poor creatures in this world, what must be the recompense reserved for them in eternity! O my God, I will keep close to you, hidden in this Sacrament; let the bitter waters of tribulation, temptation, abandonment, come, they will pass over my head, yet I shall be safe.

O Mother of holy hope! keep me day and night, by desire, if not in reality, near you, near Jesus annihilated on our altars; and I shall not be confounded, I will hope against all hope—*In Te Domine speravi, non confundar in æternam. In spe contra spem.*

THIRD VISIT.

MYSTERY OF LOVE.

Christus dilexit me—"*Christ loved me.*"

Christ loved me. O sweet words! Who could weary of hearing them? My God, You created me to love, to love You, and as nothing attracts love so much as love, You have declared, have proved Yours by every means, every sacrifice suitable to gain my heart. I therefore believe you love me, and were not all the mysteries of your Incarnation, life, death, here to convince, to attract, to charm me, there is one mystery that in some manner surpasses all—*Omnium miraculorum maximum**—and suffices for me. The Eucharist, God with us, God, immolated incessantly, God, the food of man! Oh! how well you are acquainted with this human heart created by Yourself, how amply You have provided for all its wants! Man, when he loves, desires to behold the object of his affection, to keep it, embrace it, he would wish to incorporate it with himself, and make but one being with him; and behold, You are always present on this altar, man holds You in his hands, embraces you; nay more, consumes You, You pass into his substance, You change him into Yours; man and God make but one, and the words of the royal Prophet are verified, "I have said, You are gods"—*Ego dixi, Dii estis.*

What abasement for your Divinity! what elevation to our humanity! O love, love alone could work such a prodigy. My God, what would You have me to do to make me comprehend Your love—this mystery of love?

O Mary! you who have also loved me, because Jesus Christ has loved me, teach me to return Him love for love, not as He merits, this I can never attain, but at least as much as I am able.

FOURTH VISIT.

MYSTERY OF UNION.

Ut sint unum sicut et nos—"*That they may be one, as We also are.*"

O God! You like everything that exists, and You dislike none of your works, for it is not in hatred You have established and created all things. You

* St. Thomas Aquin.

are merciful to all, because all are Yours, O God, the lover of souls!* These are the terms, full of condescension and love, by which You desired to inspire your creatures with confidence; these the prayers You dictated to the Prophets under the law of fear. What, therefore, shall we not be permitted to say under the law of love? If you love souls with so singular affection, how should they not love one another! Thus, my Lord, to effect this admirable union of hearts, You invite them to the same table, feed them with the same Bread, present them with the same Drink; behold You give them Yourself, and thus enable them to love one another with the very Heart that commands this reciprocal affection, with the Heart that loves all in general and each in particular. And after this donation of Yourself, the authority of Your word confirms the admirable end of your gifts; You have given them a new commandment, the commandment of love. They must love one another as You, their God, have loved them. They must be one family, completely united, not like human families or the unions of the world, but like the union of God Himself. This You ask the Father, You, Who cannot meet a refusal, by these wonderful words—"That they may be one, as We also are." Woe to you, O Christians! if you love not each other, if you annul by your divisions the last prayer of your God, about to die for you!

Mary, O you who have given, delivered up this well-beloved Son of the Eternal Father and your own to death, unite in your Heart, pierced with the sword of grief for us, unite friend and enemy, believer and unbeliever, Catholic and heretic, that there may be but one fold and one Shepherd.

* Wisdom ii. 24, 27.

FIFTH VISIT.

Ubi est fides tua ?—"Where is your faith?"

Where is my faith? Oh, where? People sometimes dare to say, "O my God, had You addressed to me one of those sweet words You sometimes speak to the Saints, did You give me one of those proofs of love which astonish and confound, then would my heart and flesh rejoice in You, then would I awake from this afflicting torpor." My dear Lord, where is my faith? Truly I am aware of the danger of these extraordinary favours, I desire them not. What afflicts my soul, what exasperates me against myself is, that faith does not produce in me, in Holy Communion, in the visits which I pay You, those wonderful effects operated in the Saints. I have reason to think that I approach You without respect, without fear, with heart and mind drowsy, if not asleep. In this Sacrament I have as much, even more, than You can give Your friends in the other communications of Your love, and I do not think of It, I do not appreciate It. For me only, as for Mary, as for the Saints, even the most privileged, You have taken a body—*Propter nos homines.* O God, O Jesus! whence comes it You are so powerful in them, so impotent in my soul? In Communion the miracle is worked for me alone. Oh, why, having created me to know, to love You in this mystery of condescension and love, why have You left me so stolid in sounding their depth, so cowardly in tracing in myself their humiliations, so stiff in acknowledging them by love and devotedness? Ah, Lord, I ask but faith alone, but one as entire, as lively, as active as it can be here below.

Mary, give me a ray of that light which illumined your soul, and I shall no longer be in darkness!

SIXTH VISIT.

Venite et videte opera Domini: quæ posuit prodigia super terram —"Come and behold ye the works of the Lord: what wonders He hath done upon earth" (Psalm xlv. 9).

The Holy Sacrifice, Communion, the uninterrupted Presence on our altars, admirable mysteries, each day renewed, the whole world over, in a countless number of churches! Of all who witness these prodigies, who even participate in the holy mysteries, how many search into them—are not contented to remain on the surface? How few there are who penetrate these abysses of love! How few love truly Him, Who loves them with so generous affection! O Lord, mankind knows You not; I know You not as You are. To whom do You dispense the treasures of Your power, wisdom, and love, to whom? Ah, vain is their labour. We see nothing, understand nothing, are touched by nothing, at least, not as we ought. Speak to Your Angels, to Your Saints; by us You are not heard.

O Mary, you who were surrounded with light and heat when participating in the Eucharistic mysteries, behold what darkness is ours, how icy cold our hearts! You who are so rich, despise not our poverty, have pity on our dulness, we have no heart. O sweet and compassionate above all! O sweet Mother! let not our misery repulse you. O you, who alone knew how to please our Lord Jesus Christ, cover us with the mantle of your merits!

SEVENTH VISIT.

Non est qui resistat manui ejus, et dicat ei: quare fecisti?—"And there is none that can resist His hand, and say to Him: Why hast thou done it?" (Dan. v. 32).

No, my God, You permit not proud reason to ask the motive of Your works, and he who endeavours to scrutinize Your majesty will be overwhelmed by it. But You do not refuse to submissive faith the permission humbly to ask the reason of the prodigies Your love accomplishes in this Sacrament. I therefore, though but dust and ashes, will approach your Tabernacle and say— O my Lord, *Why have you acted thus?* Why so much annihilation in this mystery? Alas! men know not how to be grateful for it. My God, allow me to say it— Have You not gone beyond the end You proposed to Yourself in keeping Yourself so hidden, so obscure, so annihilated? You desired that all should approach You without fear, but do You not risk their coming without reverence, without dread, without trying to comprehend the excess of Your abasement, Your love in this mystery? I know well You do everything with wisdom, console me then, enlighten me, explain to me how You obtain glory from a mystery whose depths few try to fathom. "One single heart that understands Me, recompenses Me for the blindness of a thousand. I explain to My friends, and according to My promise, I will discover to them My secrets." Ah, how wearisome must be my conversation, how cold my heart, how weak my faith! how You must desire to leave me! Nevertheless, I long to keep You, and never to separate from You. Pity me, teach me how to receive You, to visit You, to speak to You, to hear You, and remain inviolably united to you.

O Mary! if it were for you alone that Jesus worked this prodigy, we should not marvel, yet where could He repose since your departure from earth? Prepare my heart, all hearts, that such a Guest may never be unworthily received.

EIGHTH VISIT.

Videremus Eum sicuti est—"*We shall see Him as He is.*"

My Jesus, how did mankind behold You during the days of Your mortality? They saw You as a simple man, subject to all human miseries, they beheld You as an obscure artizan, receiving from others the price of his work. On the day of Your great sacrifice, they saw not a man, but a worm, without power, without splendour, without beauty; the outcast of the people, covered with wounds from head to foot, expiring on an infamous gibbet, in excessive pain and ignominy. This grand mystery of love—a God suffering and dying for men—confounded them, and in the pride of their hearts they *would* not recognize in You the Author of life. To the chosen people, who saw Your miracles, who had the glory of reckoning You among their fellow-citizens, the happiness of gazing on Your face, so full of grace and majesty, Your Cross was a scandal—a folly to the nations seated in the shadow of death.

And how do men see You now, O Lord? They behold You in the inexplicable secrets of Your providence, yet dare to call before the erring tribunal of their reason the God Who will be their Judge. They behold You in this Sacrament concealed, humbled under these poor species, yet so much love cannot enter into their limited understanding, their narrow hearts; they deny the blessing, or forget it, in order to dispense themselves from the gratitude due to such bounty. My God, one day all, friends and enemies, shall see You as You are, in the splendour of Your glory and power. O happy day, day of justice for You, above all, Lord, so unworthily treated, more contemned than the least of Your servants. Increase the number of those who know and honour You here below, O You, Who desire not the death of the sinner, but rather that he be converted and live for a blessed eternity.

O Mary, one day I, too, shall see You with Jesus, if the mercy of my Saviour follows me during the course of my exile. At last, one day I shall truly love You, O Jesus. O Mary, I who sigh not to be able to do it now as I desire, as I ought, this hope is my joy in affliction.

NINTH VISIT.

Fortis est ut mors dilectio—"*Love is strong as death*" (Cant. viii. 6).

Love triumphs over all difficulties, clears all barriers, overturns all obstacles; to it nothing is difficult, nothing bitter, provided it attains its end. Such has been Your love for us, my God; it has been stronger than death, which is but the sacrifice of an instant. For You, love has been a continual grief of three-and-thirty years; an uninterrupted death to all joy of mind, of heart, of sense; a death to honour, life, repose. Love makes You continue in this Sacrament the same life of incessant death. Thus, my Jesus, I hear You say to me from this tabernacle—"Seek your repose where I have found it—in death by love." O daily death, O uninterrupted death, if I do not embrace you I do not love.

If love be at this price, let us die daily, hourly. O Jesus! you leave to worldlings their frivolous joys, their insipid delights, but they are deprived of the great, the ineffable beatitude. They do not love You—You Whose affection alone merits the name, You Whose love can alone satiate the heart!

O Mary! who have loved and suffered so much, obtain that love may give me death, that death may give me love.

TENTH VISIT.

O amare! O ire! O sibi perire! O ad Deum pervenire
(St. Augustine).

These words were addressed to You, O Lord, by a heart fortunate enough to be inflamed with Your love. *O amare!*—Oh, to love! Alas! it is You alone, my Jesus, knows how to do so—only You, of Whom love is the life! Love! it is Yourself, according to the definition of the Apostle—"God is charity." *O ire!*—Oh, to go with giant strides from Heaven to the crib, from the manger to Calvary, from Calvary to this tabernacle! What steps will lead us to you? what sacrifices equal yours? *O sibi perire!*—Oh, to die to self! We shall be restored to life in coming to You. You alone had something to lose in abasing Yourself to a level with your creatures. In coming to us You have passed through successive annihilations, successive deaths, while here in this tabernacle You are in a state of continued immolation. See how You loved us!

Behold by what wonderful ways you have humbled yourself for us ! See the example You have given us to come to You; it is contained in one continuous act, in one single word—*love*. O my soul! love Him Who has so loved you, and *then* do as you please; there will be no labour, no sacrifices, no death that will not appear desirable to you. Oh, to love, to go, to die to self, to come to God !

O Mary! draw me after you ; I know not how to advance a single step. Draw me and I shall come, shall attract others, and together we shall run in the odour of your perfumes.

ELEVENTH VISIT.

Let us love, let us love.

She whom the Church has styled the Mother of beautiful love—*Mater pulchræ dilectionis*—having once appeared to the holy Armelle, said to her but these words—" Let us love, let us love." Her words were effective, for the servant of God adds —" Since that time I no longer knew myself, so ardent and penetrating was the fire of divine love." O holy Mother! say also to me these words, but say them efficaciously. O Lord Jesus, hidden in this tabernacle, command me to love You. What love for nothingness like us ! You transgress the boundaries of wisdom and reason ; shall love for You, inflaming my heart, never excite *me* beyond measure? O my dear Lord, coming so frequently into my heart, and entirely absorbing it, will You ever communicate to me that intoxication of love that consumes You and makes You languish on our altars, as formerly on the hard wood of the Cross? Will You always love without a return?

Oh, You have taught me a secret of which I shall make use. I will love You in Holy Communion with the same love with which Your Father loves You. There I possess Him with You. There He loves You. Here, in this poor, confined, unworthy, miserable temple, He acts as He does in Heaven. Here is displayed the mysterious love of the Blessed Trinity, which ravishes Heaven. Here, within me, burns this mutual love of the Father and the Son, whence proceeds the Holy Ghost. Miserable creature, what can I do? I will offer You all these flames, all this fire, as if they burned in my own heart; *my heart*, an altar frequently more a stranger to these mysteries than the material altar on which the Adorable Sacrifice is accomplished; and yet it is true that all these prodigies take place within me! O heart of mine, whilst you are in darkness all the splendour of Heaven illumines you! At sight of the marvels effected for the chosen people when leaving Egypt the mountains and hills leaped for joy; and here, why does my heart—a witness, a land of prodigies in itself—why does it not exult? Why does it not give tears to my eyes? O God! O Jesus! O Trinity of love, hidden under these species, concealed within my heart!

Mother of love, repeat for me the lesson given to your faithful servant—"Let us love, let us love!"

TWELFTH VISIT.

Quid hoc ad amorem—"What is this to love?"

O my God, what a desert for the heart, to be loved by no one in this world! But to be loved—passionately loved—by a God, and to be ignorant of it all one's life, or only to learn it when it becomes impossible to return it—what torture, what regrets it would cause! Alas! how many days and years have I lost in this fatal ignorance! My Lord, what shall I do to repair time lost? How obtain Your love, in order to be loved by You, to love You to the last moment of my life? One of Your dearest servants, in order to excite in himself contempt for things of time, was accustomed to say—" What is this or that to eternity?" And I, in order to despise all that opposes the perfect union of my heart with Yours, will henceforth say—" What is this or that to love?" Oh, how love—the desire of obtaining Your love—gives me courage for all sacrifices, for all humiliations! This, then, O my hidden Saviour, this is the compact I make with You in order to obtain the end of all my desires—Your love. I will humble myself beneath every creature, willingly, joyously, constantly, give me but Your knowledge, Your love. I will remain a stranger to all that is not You, deign but to manifest Yourself to me. I will keep silence, but You will speak; I will fly the familiarity of creatures, but You will initiate me into Your secrets; I will seek solitude, but You will bear me company; I will refuse every satisfaction to my senses, but You will be the joy of my heart.

What did I say, O my God! I am a mercenary soul, that promises sacrifices only at the price of consolation. No; I will seek You, I will follow You whatever be Your severity towards me. I merit this chastisement. Provided that I find You at the end of my pilgrimage, provided that You spare me for eternity, I consent to love You here below, without sentiment, without knowledge, only grant that I may truly love You!

S

O Mary! you who, possessing so pure love of God, yet never said—"It is enough," give me a devouring hunger, an insatiable thirst, that nothing can satisfy, so that I may run without delay to God by the generous sacrifice of all that is not Him.

THIRTEENTH VISIT.

Amor ubi est operatur; ubi non est amor non operatur—"*Where love is, it acts; where it is not, there is no action.*"

O my soul! come and learn if you love Him Who has so loved you; come and learn how you can prove to Him your love. Where are your works? You behold what Jesus has done for you, see what you have done for Him. O Lord! Your life, Your death, have been occupied with me; You have been a victim immolated for my soul; You have lived in a continued preparation for this bloody sacrifice, the most painful and ignominious one possible; and, to perpetuate this living active charity to the end of ages, You have devized the most astonishing of prodigies, You have hidden Yourself in this Host. O Lord, and what have I done? What have I suffered in return? Shall I still live in this destructive ingratitude? O You! Who give the *will*, give me the power to *do;* one is not more mine than the other. Grant that, after Your example, my entire life may be a continual immolation, both in desire and action. You gave Yourself to me covered with wounds, satiated with opprobriums, physical pains, ignominy, subjection, abasement—behold my portion, my life, if I desire to love You truly. How glorious and worthy of envy will it be should I incessantly look to You. For, if it be hard and painful to die daily to self, it is then we live in You, and what a life is that! Take, then, my Lord, Your two-edged sword, which separates the divine and human life; retrench on one side, empty on the other; give entrance into my heart to all the joys of life and death in You. Oh! it will be sweet thus to die.

Mary, by your soul transpierced with the sword of sorrow, grant that I may be firm and unshaken under the action of the spiritual sword which wounds but to heal!

FOURTEENTH VISIT.

Producam ignem in medio tui, qui comedat te—"*I will bring forth a fire from the midst of thee to devour thee*" (Ezec. xxviii. 18).

What is this fire, announced by one of Your Prophets, O Jesus! this fire which should consume us, make us at once live and die? Is it not that of which You have said—"I came to cast fire upon the earth, and what will I, but that it be enkindled"—that it should burn, should inflame all hearts?—*Ignem veni mittere in terram, et quid volo nisi ut accendatur?* This fire is the love with which You burn for us, which You desire to kindle in our hearts. This fire is Yourself, O God of Love! it is the Blessed Eucharist! O Furnace of Love! Your dwelling place is this tabernacle, it is there is lighted that divine flame in which all your true servants behold all their terrestrial bonds consumed; it is in the participation of this adorable Sacrament, they sing in the depths of their hearts a song of gratitude and praise more harmonious to Your ears than that of the Three Children. My God! if You are a fire, how comes it I am not warmed, how do I not burn when You enter into my heart? If You are a consuming fire, how does it happen that the rust of my vices resist your action? If you are a jealous God, why not command Your rivals to quit the sanctuary of my heart, where You alone should reign? My God, work this miracle. You can do it. I implore it by Your excessive love.

O Mary, you have prepared the way for Jesus in my heart. Your love has been the fire in which my chains were melted, and which made me aspire to the love of Jesus; complete your work, my Mother!

FIFTEENTH VISIT.

Rabbi, ubi habitas? Venite et videte—"*Master, where dwellest Thou? Come and see*" (St. John i. 38).

My Lord and Master, tell me where You dwell! Methinks I hear You reply with admirable sweetness, as to the two disciples of the Precursor, who first addressed this question to You—*Come and see.* But where shall I go to contemplate the magnificence of Your palace? Doubtless to Heaven, where beholding You glorious and triumphant, I shall cry out with one of Your Prophets—"O Israel, how great is the house of God, how vast the extent of His dominion! How happy are the courtiers of the Lord, who behold Him with their eyes, who dwell for ever in His presence!" But, O my Jesus, if descending from this splendour, ravished with admiration, deprived of words to express it, I come to this tabernacle, Your dwelling upon earth, what must be my astonishment, my gratitude, my love? You so great in Heaven, so little in this Host; so rich in the kingdom of glory, so poor on earth; so powerful, so honoured, so loved in Sion; so weak, so despised, so forgotten within the tabernacle!

This then is where You reside through love for me, during my exile, in order to encourage me by Your Presence, by Your example. I will dwell in heart and mind for ever with You, here in this humble abode. What would be my ingratitude if I forgot You?

O Mary, lead me back to this place of delight each time I withdraw from it; teach me to keep faithful company with that God, a thousand-fold good, Who is here shut up, inclosed for love of me.

SIXTEENTH VISIT.

Vide regnum Dei, intra vos est—" Lo, the kingdom of God is within you" (St. Luke xvii. 31).

God's kingdom is Heaven, where He reigns with the Saints and Angels in all the splendour of His glory. His kingdom is the humble dwelling He has chosen in every faithful heart still in this land of exile; it is this tabernacle in which my God has concealed Himself to dwell with men. Where the King is, there is His court. I find here, therefore, all that I hope for in Heaven; I shall there behold nothing I do not now believe with steadfast faith. The Heavenly object of my love, He Who delights the Saints in the eternal abode of charity, I possess here in this Sacrament. The better I shall know Him here, the more I shall understand Him in the holy city; the more I shall love Him in exile, the more fully shall I contemplate Him in Sion. O my Lord Jesus, I know not why, how much You have loved those who preceded me, how much You love those who surround me. Oh! speak to me, teach me what I can do to love You at least as much as a heart so miserable and imperfect as mine can.

O Mary, give me your love for Jesus; establish His kingdom in me on the ruins of all that belongs not to Him.

SEVENTEENTH VISIT.

Et ipse solus in terra—"*And Himself alone on the land*"
(St. Mark vi. 47).

Bound, embarrassed, drawn away by all the vain creatures that surround me, I take refuge with You, my Jesus, hidden in this Sacrament; in You, Whose regards alone should attract mine, Whose sole approbation should satisfy my heart, Whose conversation alone should be my solace in the weariness of this world, as it shall be the reward of my labours in Heaven. I come to rest from my vain pursuits, from my childish human respects in this peaceful thought— There is but You "alone on the land." What is all beside? The grain of sand in the balance, the trace of a ship on the waters, an empty sound, a shadow; to Your eyes all things are as if they were not. O my God, there is but You and I "on the land." O profound, extensive, delightful solitude! May I ever dwell therein. You alone are mine, are for me. All seek their own interests, their own satisfaction—You alone have loved me even before my existence. Who could have done so but You? You alone have followed every movement of mine with loving and jealous eyes, without a moment's forgetfulness of Your wretched creature. You alone will love me and perpetuate my life with Yourself in Heaven. O my Jesus, *there is but You;* I am nothing, can be nothing but in You. I have long known this, yet acted as if I were ignorant of it. Through this love, hidden for me in the depths of the tabernacle, pardon me; and as there is but You alone to defend me, You alone Who truly love me, grant also that there may be but You alone for me, but You alone in my heart.

Mary, O you, for whom Jesus was really *all in all*, come to my aid, hasten to assist me; for ever, for ever close my eyes, my ears, my heart to all that is not God.

EIGHTEENTH VISIT.

Pars mea Deus in æternum—"*My portion for ever*" *is God*
(Psalm lxxii. 26).

O Jesus, You have put these beautiful words in the mouth of one of Your Prophets, and I dare to repeat after him—God is "my portion for ever." How glorious, how advantageous has destiny been to me! My soul, rejoice with exceeding great joy! You that nothing can satiate, nothing fulfil your desires, shall at length be satisfied; God will be your immense, your only Good. He will belong to you unveiled in Heaven. He is yours on earth, hidden in this Sacrament. Behold the wealth which all can share with you, without the slightest diminution of its greatness; wealth of which none can deprive you. A blissful eternity is mine in this tabernacle; I can enjoy it in advance, can begin it in my exile. I have, then, nothing to envy the rich, the great, the happy of the world; nothing to deplore in the losses and disgraces that occur. I have my hidden God on the altar for riches, happiness, consolation. Without Him, of what value is all that ends with time?

Mary, you also are my portion for eternity, you on earth, you in Heaven with Jesus, "and I am rich enough, I desire nothing more."

NINETEENTH VISIT.

Numquid possunt filii sponsi lugere quamdiu cum illis est sponsus?—"Can the children of the Bridegroom mourn as long as the Bridegroom is with them?"

It is not alone Your Prophets speaking in Your name, but Yourself, my Jesus, Who, with Your own divine lips, console me from this tabernacle. It is You Who pronounce these sweet, paternal words, formerly uttered by You, while residing upon earth, "Can the children of the Bridegroom mourn as long as the Bridegroom is with them?" And as I know, as You have said, that You will abide in this Sacrament till the end of time, I shall therefore be always happy; I shall always find in You happiness in the midst of weeping, joy even in the depth of affliction. But to attain this end, my God, I must remain with You, for if I leave You, I shall find tribulation and grief. Ah! how often have I encountered them in just punishment of my inconstancy in keeping close to the tabernacle! My Jesus, let me never be separated from You—*Ne permittas me separari a Te.* Come, come, and let me never withdraw from You. You are sufficient for me; You alone console me for everything.

O Mary! after Jesus, you are the consolation of the afflicted. In all my tribulations I will remember you; I will remember Jesus and be consoled—*Memor fui Dei et consolatus sum.*

TWENTIETH VISIT.

Pauper servus et humilis manducat Dominum!—"The humble and poor servant eats his Master!"

Behold, my heart, the most incomprehensible of mysteries! O my God, what have You invented in the excess of Your love? If, at least, men received You into their souls, if they consumed their Lord with an avidity corresponding to the love with which You give Yourself! O Jesus, what have You done? To descend from Heaven, to astonish the celestial court, to multiply prodigies: annihilation, inexplicable love; and why? That you might enter a heart, cold, distracted, erring, which thanks You not, loves You not, asks nothing from You, is not enchanted at Your entrance, or grieved at Your departure! Who would believe it? How Your Heart must be wounded! O Jesus, when You come into my poor heart, touch it, wound it, soften it by an inexhaustible gift of tears. Come into this heart, and enkindle therein the furnace of a continual and ever-increasing love. I offer You, in atonement for my inability, all the tears that flowed from Your Divine Eyes, all those of Your Blessed Mother, and of all mankind. I offer You all the ardour of Your Sacred Heart, of the Heart of Mary, of the Saints, of all Your creatures, friends and enemies. Oh! why cannot I shed all these tears myself? They would be insufficient to cleanse my impure soul, to efface the shameful stain of my persevering ingratitude. Why can I not enkindle all these fires in my heart? They would not suffice to return your burning love. And I can do nothing! I do nothing!

O Mary! give me your Heart to receive my tears; mine is and always shall be unworthy to do so!

TWENTY-FIRST VISIT.

Non sic sancti Tui, non sic—"*No, no, it was not thus that Your Saints loved.*"

My Lord, and my God, it is with confusion and grief of heart I come to Your feet, I dare to approach You in this tabernacle. Most frequently I present myself with a heart unmoved, with distraction of mind. Time appears long, and I retire without asking anything, without having loved, praised, or thanked You. Ah, it was not so Your dear friends approached You, those Saints of all ages, whose admirable lives are a condemnation of my tepid and slothful one. Alas! when I remember the fervour with which they visited You, the effort it cost them to withdraw from the holy altar, I know not how to excuse myself, or how You can suffer me near You. O my merciful Lord, can I hope one day to love You, I who act in no way as Your Saints, who bear nothing for Him Who has suffered so much for me? My God, *I too* desire to love You! Pardon me, animate me, for the sake of Your friends reject me not, turn not away Your face from me!

O Mary, you who above all, during your mortal life, after the Ascension of your Divine Son, found your repose and joy only in the Sacrament—for sake of this beloved Son, for your own sake, whom my coldness grieves, give me a heart capable of making some return of love to Jesus, annihilated for me under the sacred species.

TWENTY-SECOND VISIT.

Sitio—"*I thirst*" (St. John xix. 28).

I approach You, my Jesus, and seem to hear from the depth of the tabernacle Your voice, still repeating—"*I thirst*. I thirst for your love, for the sacrifices you ought to impose on yourself. O beloved soul, will you never tell Me that you also thirst for Me? Up to this you have given Me but tepid progress and imperfect sacrifices in return for the ardour that consumes Me." O my God, say once again to my heart this word uttered on the Cross. Yes, for me as for Your souls of predilection, say—*I thirst* I thirst for you! Oh, what love! make me understand it. Oh, give me this thirst corresponding to Your own, this thirst that makes Your true friends. What is that fountain of living water, that spring whence issue impetuously those waters that quench the thirst of those who languish with this desire? *Emanaverunt putei aquarum*—" Wells of water flowed."

It is Your Heart, O Jesus, inclosed within this tabernacle, fatigued with following, weary waiting for my soul so long, and saying to me, Oh, "if thou didst know the gift of God"—*Se scires donum Dei!* The Gift of God is He Whom the Father hath given us in the excess of His love—"For God so loved the world as to give His only-begotten Son."[*] And is not He Who gives pleased to see His gifts well received, made much of, taken possession of? My God, I receive You from the hands of Your Father; You are mine, since this is Your Father's desire, this is Your own gracious will. I come, I prostrate myself before You, I approach Your Sacred Heart, I receive You into mine, and I also say—"Give me to drink"— *Da mihi bibere,*[†] for I thirst for You, only for You, and the oftener I receive You, the more do I thirst.

O Mary, you who lived and died incessantly of this thirst, perpetually renewed, perpetually satisfied, give me your eagerness, give me of your fulness!

[*] St. John iii. 16. [†] St. John iv. 7.

TWENTY-THIRD VISIT.

Misereor super turbam quia ecce jam triduo sustinent Me, nec habent quod manducent—"*I have compassion on the multitude, for behold they have been with Me three days, and have nothing to eat* (St. Mark viii. 2).

My Jesus, hidden in this Sacrament, explain to me what must have been the charm of Your words, the sweetness and majesty of Your countenance, the authority and secret influence of Your love, thus to attract a blind and ignorant multitude, and cause them to forget for days and nights the most imperative wants of nature. What did you not teach them in the desert! With what zeal was Your Heart inflamed, seeing these poor sheep without a shepherd! O my Jesus, repeat to me all the lessons You taught them; tell me how the days and nights passed so rapidly with You. I have the same attraction, the same Master as they, here, in Your Sacrament, in prayer, in Holy Communion; I possess the same God, approach yet nearer to Him; I also repose at His feet, I look at Him, I hear Him, I speak to Him—yet more, He comes into my heart; but how ill I employ this time so precious; how incapable I should be of consecrating two whole days and nights without interruption to Him like these poor people. Oh, I am not worthy of Your love, Your looks, Your conversation, Yourself! But if now, O Lord, I also desire to make You King—King of my heart—You will not fly from me, because You desire nothing so much.

Mary, behold I also am a sheep without a pastor whenever I depart from our Lord Jesus. Excite in His Heart the tender compassion with which this poor people animated Him. Implore Him to repeat incessantly to my soul that *Misereor*—" I have compassion," which creates penitents, saints, elect.

TWENTY-FOURTH VISIT.

Unde ememus panes ut manducent hi?—" *Whence shall we buy bread that these may eat?*" (St. John vi. 5).

My God, I shall not address the same question to You as Your Apostle did. When he put it, You had not yet invented that prodigy of love which we enjoy under the law of grace. One Bread alone suffices me, supplies all my wants—the Eucharistic Bread Which is found here at whatever hour I present myself. It is in You I seek, from You I expect, this Bread of truth, of love—Your Divinity, your Humanity—for the sustenance of my soul. It is from Your Wounds, from Your open Heart, from this loving and vivifying Host hidden in the tabernacle, that I seek my food. Come Yourself into my soul, enrich it, fatten it, that out of Your abundance it may be able to give to those dependent on it—to the souls of my parents, friends, servants. These souls are Yours, they are mine; You gave them to me—protect Your property, this property shared in common with me, unworthy though I be. Truly You must look upon my soul as your spouse, since You share with me your most precious treasure—souls. My God, that I may be useful to them, never leave us; let my heart be Yours, my hand be in Yours while I labour here. I want but You, I desire but You for myself, and all I love in You.

O Mary, give me Jesus, give me to Jesus, and I wish for nothing more!

T

TWENTY-FIFTH VISIT.

Pueri numquid pulmentarium habetis?—"*Children have you any meat?*" (St. John xxi. 5).

My God, You ask this question because You desire to fill me. Would a rich man thus interrogate the poor without designing to help him? It would be a cruel irony to the misery of the unfortunate. Would a God ask it of His poor creature, and then leave him in hunger and thirst? You are too good to treat me with so great harshness, too great to insult the poverty of a worm of the earth that implores Your pity. Did I behold an abandoned child whose cries appealed to my assistance, I should be the more compassionate as he knew not the whole extent of his misery. Before You I am as this poor orphan, who knows not his abandonment, understands not Your language, knows You not, is not aware of his wants. Oh, through pity then, look on me, assist me, nourish me. The food necessary for me, the nourishment prepared for the poor by Your kindness is hidden here in the tabernacle; come forth, my Lord, come into my heart! Come, for I am dying of hunger! Come Yourself, for all You give me without Yourself is nothing, cannot satisfy my soul.

O Mary, give me of your Bread, the Bread you destined for me, the Wine that alone can rejoice my heart, "and I have nothing more to ask."

TWENTY-SIXTH VISIT.

Comedite, amici, et inebriamini charrissimi—"*Eat, O My friends, and be inebriated, My dearly beloved*" (Cant. v. 1).

This is Your invitation to me from the place of Your concealment. And the Seraphic Doctor, commenting on these tender words, tells us—" All friends dirnk of this wine, but the beloved are inebriated therewith." My Lord, if it be so pleasing to breathe the perfume of Your sweetness, what will it be to taste thereof? If he who only approaches his lips finds such strength, what shall be said of him who fully gratifies his desire? Oh, I must confess, it is not enough to feel the distant perfume of Your sweetness, nor even to taste it with measure, I desire to be inebriated. Oh, who will give me to have You in my heart, to be filled with the wine of Your love, to embrace You, O my God. I know that the Spouse says—" Drink My friends, and be inebriated, My dearly beloved." If the wretched soul that implores the favour of being reckoned among the dearest friends of God is unworthy that favour, He that proposes it is so good, I dare hope to obtain it. Can I doubt that He Who disdained not to suffer for me will also be ready to share with me His wealth?* Has He not given me the pledge, the fulfilment of it in this Sacrament, in this Heavenly Manna, which contains in itself all delights, as the Church sings—*Panem de cælo præstitisti eis, omne delectamentum in se habentem* —" Thou hast given them Bread from Heaven, replenished with all delights."

Give me to love You, O Jesus, annihilated for love of me, grant me Your love. Burst all barriers, let Your love inundate my soul. O You, Whom day and night I alone desire, Come! come!

O Mary, the most loving and most beloved of creatures, teach me daily, hourly, what I should do and suffer to obtain the immense favour of being counted not only among the friends, but even among the *dearest friends* of Jesus.

* St. Bonaventure, *Sol.*

TWENTY-SEVENTH VISIT.

Vanitas vanitatum et omnia vanitas—"*Vanity of vanities and all is vanity*" (Eccles. i. 2).

My soul, wearied with useless labours, comes to You buried in this tabernacle, O Jesus, to obtain comfort by relating her vexations. O Lord, support of my weakness, repairer of my falls, where am I going? How do my days, my hours, my years pass? Life glides on, at a distance from You, in trifles which afflict me. This rapid river called time I allow to glide and overflow the land. It is lost, instead of joining You, O great Ocean, in which all is again found. Will You not pity my misery, my helplessness? My soul flies towards You with impetuous desires, then falls again to earth, where nothing can satisfy her. All outside of You is vanity—vanity and folly. The affection, the conversation of creatures, vanity; their praises, vanity; science and labour, vanity; repose, joy, sorrow, all that is not You, undertaken, suffered for You, vanity, folly, misery. Yet by these well known snares I allow myself to be taken daily! Oh, who will deliver me from this death that is called life? Your love, Your love alone. Holy Father, give me the love of Jesus; I implore it through Jesus, Who solicits it for me with extended and suppliant arms, nailed to the Cross; through Jesus, Who remains a Victim in this Sacrament only to gain hearts.

Mary obtain this grace for me containing every other—*to love Jesus even to hatred of self.* O you, who only consoled yourself for the labours rendered by your Divine Son in the thought of the grateful love of mankind, listen to me, hear me favourably.

TWENTY-EIGHTH VISIT.

Vulnerasti cor meum, soror mea sponsa; vulnerasti cor meum in uno oculorum tuorum, et in uno crine colli tui—" *Thou wounded My heart, My sister, My spouse; thou hast wounded My heart with one of thy eyes, with one hair of thy neck*" (Cant. iv. 9).

O my God, is it possible a slight victory obtained over my passions, less even than that, a look, a tear is enough, not only to appease Your indignation, but to touch You, to wound Your Heart, to delight It. And as for me, Lord — Your thorns, Your nails, Your lance, Your bloody sweat, Your continued captivity in this Sacrament, so many prodigies of love, cannot wound my heart. Of what nature can it be? Yours so tender, mine so hard. You do so much—You, the God, the Lord of my soul—yet exact so little. My Jesus, what must be your thoughts when with burning Heart You enter my frozen one; when Your members, covered with wounds, are united to my unmortified ones? Oh, say not in Your indignation —"*Let us go hence*, let us go hence;" but teach me how to prove my love for You, as You have proved Your own for me.

O Jesus, O Mary, may every act, word, and suffering of Yours be as so many inflamed darts incessantly transpiercing my heart. You can do this, and why should You not will it?

TWENTY-NINTH VISIT.

Deus, propitius esto mihi peccatori!—"*O God, be merciful to me a sinner!*" (St. Luke xviii. 13).

O good and compassionate Jesus, in Heaven Your greatness affrights me; but in this Sacrament Your incomprehensible abasement reassures

TWENTY-EIGHTH VISIT

...the
...is
...feel
...and
...the pro-
...When I
...govern
...through
...recall it;
...as a
...is an
...their
...of existence.
...work, business,
...Life is so short.
...to find You as
...midst of all the
...You come to me
...rament, allow me
...least to pay You
...cannot give You
...mortal life, nothing
...Your Divine Father
...sadness, nothing
...wish me to imitate
...cept—"If any one
...let him . . . follow
...hat You command.
...You, as You were
...al life, as You are
...ment. O Divine
...Holy Body

me and gives me the hardihood to speak to You heart to Heart.

My Lord and my God, what would become of me if, calling me before Your tribunal, You compared my life, not to Your own, but only to that of Your Saints? Oh, what would I do, what present to You? Barren desires—no actions. How should I act? What do You desire of me? Have You exhausted all the treasures of Your charity on the Saints? My Lord and my God, I will not have the boldness to demand the gold and precious stones with which You enrich Your faithful spouses. Oh, give to this wretched beggar, who waits in silence and confusion, turning towards You many imploring looks; give the mendicant a little bread, a drop of water; give, not the crumbs of Your Divine Table—of that Table, at which Your dear friends are satiated—but some of the bread reserved for the domestics, the animals. Provided I obtain it from Your hands, I shall be but too honoured. Give me for the refreshment of my heart one of Your tears; a drop of that water that issued from Your wounded Side.

Oh, hold me by the hand without my feeling it; look at me without my perceiving it; love me through compassion, without my knowledge; carry me in Your arms, unconsciously to me; but save me, "be merciful to me a sinner," to me, the least of Your creatures, because the most ungrateful.

O Mary, the more compassionate as we are more miserable, pray for me a poor sinner, now, always, and especially at the hour of my death.

THIRTIETH VISIT.

De profundis clamavi ad Te Domine—"*Out of the depths have I cried to Thee, O Lord*" (Psalm cxxix. 1).

My Lord Jesus, it is to You I come to seek the remedy for all my pains. What unhappiness is mine. You alone know it; You alone can feel that all-powerful compassion that consoles and heals. O my God, hear my sighs from the profound abyss in which I am plunged. When I desire to go to You, why can I not even govern my thoughts? My imagination wanders through unknown ways, from which it is difficult to recall it; this corruptible body, which You have given as a prison to my soul, weighs it down, and is an obstacle to finding You. The senses and their attractions carry away the most part of existence. Health, sickness, preoccupation of work, business, all stops my way towards You, and life is so short. O my God, when shall I be able to find You as Your Saints have done in the midst of all the embarrassments of life? Since You come to me in this life in the Blessed Sacrament, allow me to go to You; permit me at least to pay You attention for attention, since I cannot give You love for love. During Your mortal life, nothing could interrupt Your union with Your Divine Father —labours, sorrows, tortures, joy, sadness, nothing separated you from Him. You wish me to imitate You; it is You Who gave the precept—" If any one will come after Me, . . . let him . . . follow Me." My God, do with me what You command. Let me be incessantly united to You, as You were to Your Father during Your mortal life, as You are still united to Him in this Sacrament. O Divine Body, most pure Body, most holy Body, that followed most faithfully all the impulses of the most beautiful and generous Soul that ever existed, I adore and invoke You; quicken, purify, sanctify my body and soul.

O Mary, I give myself up to you, in order that you may obtain from Jesus that He would vouchsafe to reform my body and soul after the model of yours while on earth, yet awaiting the day when He will reform them after the model of His glorified Body.

THIRTY-FIRST VISIT.

Vivam ego, jam non ego; vivat vero in me Christus—"*I live, now not I; but Christ liveth in me*" (Gal. ii. 20).

Is it asking too much thus to live, my Jesus? Ah, no; since it was that weak and miserable man might live the same life as God, that the God of power and greatness became Man, mortal and capable of suffering. Lord Jesus, may then Your will be done. May I live with You, in You, by You; may You alone live in me. O Jesus, renew in my heart, through this mystery of Love, the Eucharist, all You did during Your mortal life. Come dwell in my heart; there be born, there weep, pray, fast; there keep silence, there speak, heal all the maladies of my soul; repeat again all the instructions of Your three years in Palestine; look at me, listen to me, touch me; there sigh, sweat blood, enter into an agony; there accomplish all the mysteries of Your Passion and Resurrection. O my Life, live in me, and permit me not to die of hunger, thirst, and weariness, away from You.

O Mary, you whose life was a reflection of that of Jesus, obtain for me, that I may be another Christ—*Christianus alter Christus.*

Anima Christi.

(To be said after each Visit.)

Three hundred days' Indulgence for each recital. Seven years and seven quarantines to all Priests who say it after Mass, or to the Faithful after Holy Communion. (Pope Pius IX. January 9th, 1854.)

Soul of Christ be my sanctification;
Body of Christ be my salvation;
Blood of Christ fill all my veins;
Water of Christ's Side, wash out my stains;
Passion of Christ my comfort be;
O good Jesus listen to me;
In Thy Wounds I fain would hide,
Ne'er to be parted from Thy Side;
Guard me, should the foe assail me;
Call me when my life shall fail me;
Bid me come to Thee above,
With Thy Saints to sing Thy love
   World without end. Amen.*

Short Act of Consecration to the Sacred Heart of Jesus.

Jesus, my God, my King, and most amiable Master, with the design of rendering all the homage that I can to Your Sacred Heart, consumed with love for me, I vow and consecrate to this Divine Heart all that I have and all that I am: my body and my soul, my memory and my understanding, my liberty and my will, my heart and all its affections, all my pains and sufferings, all my consolations and good works, all my merit present and future, for time and eternity. Amen.†

* *Raccolta.*   † Father de Ravignan, S.J.

May the Sacred Heart of Jesus be everywhere loved! (One hundred days.)

Memorare.

Remember, O most gracious Virgin Mary, that it has never yet been heard that any one who had recourse to thy patronage, invoked thy help, implored thy intercession, was left by thee unpitied and forsaken. To thee, then, most Blessed Virgin, Mother of Virgins, I fly for refuge with unbounded confidence. Behold me with a bruised and penitent heart in supplication at thy feet! Despise not my humble prayer, but hear me with pity. O Mother of Jesus, graciously hear me. Amen.

Three hundred days' Indulgence each time. Plenary Indulgence if said daily for a month on the usual conditions. Granted by Pope Pius IX., 25th July, 1846.

O Domina Mea.

Hail Mary, &c.

My Queen, my Mother! I give thee all myself; and to show my devotion to thee, I consecrate to thee this day, and for ever, eyes, ears, mouth, heart, myself wholly and without reserve. Wherefore, good Mother, as I am thine own, keep me, guard me, as a thing of thine, thine own possession.

Ejaculation.

My Queen, my Mother! remember I am thine own, keep me, guard me, as a thing of thine, thine own possession.

One hundred days' Indulgence to be gained once a day by saying morning and evening, with a "Hail Mary," the above prayer. Forty days every time when assaulted by temptation one shall say the *Ejaculation*. Plenary Indulgence if this Devotion be kept up for a month together, on the usual conditions. (5th August, 1851.)

Ave Maria Stella.

Bright Mother of our Maker, hail,
    Thou Virgin ever blest;
The ocean's Star by which we sail,
    And gain the port of rest.

While we this "Hail," address'd to thee
    From Gabriel's mouth, rehearse,
Obtain that peace our lot may be,
    And Eva's name reverse.

Release our long-entangled mind
    From all the snares of ill;
With heavenly light instruct the blind,
    And all our vows fulfil.

Exert for us a Mother's care,
    And us thy children own,
Prevail with Him to hear our pray'r,
    Who chose to be thy Son.

O spotless Maid, whose virtues shine,
    From all suspicion free;
Each action of our lives refine,
    And make us pure like thee.

Preserve our lives unstained with ill
    In this infectious way,
That Heav'n alone our souls may fill
    With joys that ne'er decay.

To God the Father, endless praise;
    To God the Son the same,
And Holy Ghost, Whose equal rays
    One equal glory claim. Amen.

Prayer to our Lady of Sorrows.

O most desolate of Mothers! what sword most terrible hath penetrated thy soul? Each blow which Jesus received in His Passion reached thee; all His sorrows depressed thy heart, and particularly the last adieu He addressed to thee, reopened all thy wounds. O Mother of grief and love, I come to entreat thy intercession, convinced of my unworthiness to obtain aught, and beseeching thee in the Name of Jesus and through thy love for His Divine Heart in the adorable Sacrament of the Altar, to beg for me my intentions. . . . . Remember, O Queen of Heaven, thy honour and that of Jesus are here concerned, and it is impossible to ask thus and ask in vain. Amen.

To all who say the "Hail Mary" seven times, with the following Versicle after each, three hundred days' Indulgence are granted, once a day, by Pope Pius VII., December 1, 1815.

> Holy Mother pierce me through,
> In my heart each wound renew
> Of my Saviour crucified.

A Prayer to be said every Day during May.

O most august and Blessed Virgin Mary, Holy Mother of God! glorious Queen of Heaven and earth! powerful protectress of those who love thee, and unfailing advocate of all who invoke thee! look down I beseech thee from thy throne of glory on thy devoted child; accept the solemn offering I present to thee of this month, specially dedicated to thee, and receive my ardent, humble desire that, by my love and fervour, I could worthily honour thee, who, next to God, art deserving of all honour. Receive me, O Mother of Mercy, among thy best beloved children; extend to me thy maternal tenderness and solicitude; obtain for me a place in the Sacred Heart of Jesus, and a special share in the gifts of His grace. Oh, deign, I beseech thee, to recognize my claims on thy protection; to watch over my spiritual and temporal interests, as well as those of all who are dear to me; to infuse into my soul the Spirit of Christ; and to teach me thyself to become meek, humble, charitable, patient, and submissive to the will of God. May my heart burn with the love of thy Divine Son, and of thee, His Blessed Mother, not for a month alone, but for time and eternity; may I thirst for the promotion of His honour and of thine, and contribute as far as I can to its extension. Receive me, O Mary, the Refuge of Sinners. Grant me a Mother's blessing and a Mother's care, now, and at the hour of my death. Amen.

Exercise to unite oneself to the Passion during the Holy Sacrifice of the Mass.

Translated from "Pratique de l'amour envers le Cœur de Jésus."

CHRISTIAN SOUL, hear Jesus Christ, Who says to you—Each time that you shall do these things, do them "for a commemoration of Me." That is, be not contented with thinking from time to time of My sufferings and death, but whenever you assist at the Divine Sacrifice, remember Me, remember that it is the testament of your dying Father, remember under what circumstances I instituted it, what agony and sufferings it should recall to you. Never retire from it without having searched into the mystery of the Passion, a mystery which excites the admiration of the Angels and Saints in Heaven. Come and see if there is any sorrow like unto My sorrow—*Attendite et videte si est dolor sicut dolor Meus.* What, would you be more tired of considering My sufferings than I Who endure them for you? Is a daily remembrance too much in return for so many ignominies, so much love?

At the beginning of Mass.

The Priest, at the foot of the Altar, represents the Agony of Jesus in the Garden of Olives.

Jesus Christ.—You who come to assist at My Sacrifice, "Stay you here and watch" with Me—*Sustinete hic, et vigilate Mecum,* withdrawing from your mind every thought foreign to the affliction of heart and mind which I endure for you. Weariness, disgust, seizes upon Me at the view of your inconstancy; I shudder with dread and horror at the consideration of the offended justice of My Father, which you do not seem to fear—*Cœpit pavere.* A mortal sadness overwhelms me when I behold the inutility of My sufferings for your perfection, for the salvation of souls dearer to Me than My own life. My Soul is sorrowful, even unto death—*Tristis est anima mea usque ad mortem.* Father, if it be possible, let this chalice pass from Me. I accept sufferings, but give Me souls purchased with such anguish.

Enter into your Saviour's Heart oppressed with these thoughts. Behold in this Heart the share you have added *yourself* to so many griefs by your own offences, which He counts one by one. Kiss the earth purpled with the Blood of your Divine Master; pray by His side, endeavouring to imitate His interior and exterior recollection.

O my Saviour, I accept the fatigues, the sadness, the fears that so frequently assail me in this melancholy life. I submit to your will: however severe it may appear to me, will it equal in rigour that of Your Father towards You? My good Jesus, by Your agony, save souls; save mine. I am sorry for having offended You; I implore Your compassion and mercy; I implore the intercession of Mary and of Your Saints.

The Priest ascends the Altar and kisses it.

Jesus strengthened but not consoled by His three hours' prayer says to His Apostles, Arise, let us go hence — Surgite eamus. He presents Himself to His enemies.

O my Divine Jesus, You had said and now You prove it, that no one could deprive You of life; love alone can take it from You; it is Yourself Who freely give and sacrifice it for us. You await not the arrival of Your enemies, You prevent them; You allow Yourself to be embraced by the traitor Judas, bound by his satellites, and shamefully dragged as a vile criminal.

O my Saviour, I also would come to You, not like Your enemies to keep You captive, but as You come to me, with a loving heart. It is You, it is Jesus of Nazareth Whom I seek. Let me hear those sweet words, "I am He"—*Ego sum*. May they cause me to fall at Your feet with feelings of regret, love, and gratitude. Permit me to kiss those chains by which You are fastened; may they bind me to You in such a manner that I can never break them; may I follow after You even through the severest trials Your divine will may appoint me to suffer.

At the Introit.

Jesus is dragged from tribunal to tribunal; before Annas, Caiphas, Pilate, Herod, again before Pilate.

Hatred, jealousy, human respect, ambition, are the real enemies that condemn You, O my Saviour, by the mouths of Your accusers, and these iniquitous judges before whom You deign to appear! Destroy in my heart these criminal passions. May they never more have the boldness to transfer You to their tribunals, to pronounce against You. They clothe You with a white robe, symbol of innocence. Ah! You alone are just, we are all culpable; we merit the contempt of creatures; I accept it, O my Jesus! I desire to be indifferent to it; I wish to be esteemed by You alone, to esteem only You. To be loved by You, to love You alone, is my only ambition.

Gloria in Excelsis.

Whilst they insult You on earth, O my Jesus, the Angels of peace weep bitterly over so many outrages—*Angeli pacis amare flebant.** They weep for our insensibility; Mary weeps for her ungrateful children; and I, the cause of so many tears, shall I never deplore my obduracy, my infidelity? They weep, but they also give glory to God, now appeased; they praise Him, they bless Him for us, who outrage and forget Him.

Dominus vobiscum.

Jesus looks at Peter.

My Jesus, what weakness is ours; how can our devotedness, or the firmness of our resolutions be counted upon? Peter, the most ardent of the Apostles, who acknowledged You as Son of the living God, who protested that though all should abandon You, he would follow You; Peter, who has just received You for the first time into his heart, swears with an oath, with imprecations, that he knows You not, that he knows not *the Man.* *The Man!* O disdainful word, word painful to Your Heart, my Jesus! You heard it, and yet, instead of being angry at so much ingratitude, at such cowardly apostasy, You look at the unfaithful

---

* Isaias.

Apostle, but with a look so merciful, so tender, so powerful, that he shall never cease henceforth to weep his fault. O my Divine Jesus, leave me not an instant to my own weakness; look at me, too, when I shall have displeased You, or rather, never take Your eyes off me, those eyes one look of which suffices to make Elect, Saints. May I also incessantly fix the eyes of my soul on You, my suffering Jesus, thus to be able to return without interruption Your loving and continual regard.

The Epistle.

Jesus accused by false witnesses.

In what insulting terms are You loaded with injuries by those blind enemies; You, the God of majesty and glory, an impostor, a seditious person. Falsehood and calumny are their only arms against Him, Who had formerly said to them, "Which of you shall convince Me of sin?" They question You, yet when You answer they are exasperated, and become so enraged as to strike that Divine Face, Whose majesty and sweetness should have commanded their respect and love. O my Jesus, who can now complain of the injustice of men? who can rely upon innocence as a justification? You desired to be here the example and the consolation of Your friends whom the world accuses, misunderstands, judges, and despises.

Epistle (Isaias, chap. liii.).—"And He shall grow up as a tender plant before Him, and as a root out of thirsty ground: there is no beauty in Him, nor comeliness: and we have seen Him, and there was no sightliness, that we should be desirous of Him. Despised, and the most abject of men, a Man of sorrows, and acquainted with infirmity, and His look was as it were hidden and despised, whereupon we esteemed Him not. Surely He hath borne our infirmities, and carried our sorrows: and we have thought Him as it were a leper, and as one struck by God and afflicted. But He was wounded for our iniquities, He was bruised for our sins: the chastisement of our peace was upon Him, and by His bruises we are healed. All we like sheep have gone astray, every one hath turned aside into his own way: and the Lord hath laid on Him the iniquities of us all. He was offered because it was His own will, and He opened not His mouth: He shall be led as a sheep to the slaughter, and shall be dumb as a lamb before His shearer, and He shall not open His mouth. He was taken away from distress and from judgment: who shall declare His generation? Because He is cut off out of the land of the living: for the wickedness of My people have I struck Him. And He shall give the ungodly for His burial and the rich for His death: because He hath done no iniquity, neither was there deceit in His mouth. And the Lord was pleased to bruise Him in His infirmity: if He shall lay down His life for sin, He shall see a long-lived seed, and the will of the Lord shall be prosperous in His hand."

At the Gospel.

Pilate delivers Jesus to be scourged; the executioners without mercy lay hold of their Victim, and cease not their blows on His open wounds until they behold Him expiring.

Consider, see this Divine Lamb with the eyes of faith, fallen through weakness at the foot of the pillar and bathed in His Blood. He says to you—"Follow Me, follow in My bloody steps. The

Kingdom of Heaven suffers violence, only the violent bear it away. Strive to enter by the narrow gate. Crucify your flesh and its unruly passions. You have not yet resisted unto blood for me. Unless you do penance you shall all perish. You call me Master and Lord, and you say well, for so I am. The servant is not greater than his Lord. If the enemies of My name have thus treated Me, they will treat you in like manner. They will persecute you, they will separate you, and say falsely all sorts of evil of you, they will drive you from their assemblies; but rejoice then and exult for joy, because a great recompense is reserved for you in Heaven."

At the Creed.

Follow in spirit the soldiers who drag Christ to the Pretorium. They strip Him of His clothes, put on Him a purple rag, and, plaiting a crown of thorns, put it on His head. They place a reed in His hand, and bowing the knee in derision say—" Hail! King of the Jews." They spit in His face, they blindfold Him, strike Him, saying—" Prophesy unto us, who is he that struck Thee?" They snatch the reed out of His hand and strike Him on the head. Yet He that is thus treated is He Whom you acknowledge as your God.

Go forth, daughter of Jerusalem, Christian soul, come and see your King ornamented with the diadem, with which His mother the Synagogue has crowned Him, on the day of His espousals, and of the joy of His Heart. O my Divine Jesus! it is now I recognize You for my King, the King of my heart. I adore You humbly prostrate at Your feet, desiring to repair so many outrages by my humiliation and my love. Should not delicate members blush under a Head crowned with thorns, the proud and haughty under a King so humble, the lovers of luxury and pleasure in the train of a Master satiated with opprobrium and pain?

At the Offertory.

Jesus is shown to the people crowned with thorns, wearing the purple mantle, and Pilate says, "Behold the Man"—Ecce Homo.

Behold the Man! See, O man, the state to which you deserve to be reduced. Behold, my soul, how you have treated the God Who for your love deigned to become Man. Behold Him Who has taken upon Him your infirmities, your weakness, your griefs, your pains; will you not adore, love, and imitate Him? O my Jesus, I see You all disfigured, all covered with blood, and will I suffer nothing?

At the Lavabo.

Pilate finds Jesus innocent: to deliver Him he presumes to place Him in competition with Barabbas; yielding to the cries of the Jews, at the fear of being declared Cæsar's enemy, he contents himself with washing his hands, to testify that he did not participate in the death of the Just Man; and he delivers Him to His enemies. The people cry out—"Away with Him! Crucify Him; He is guilty of death. . . . His Blood be upon us."

O Jesus, was it not You that had healed their sick, given sight to their blind, speech to their dumb, raised their dead to life, and Whom, in the transports of a just admiration, they wished to proclaim King? And yet they prefer a public malefactor to You. "Whether will you of the two to be released unto you, Jesus or Barabbas? Not this Man, but Barabbas." Where are now the infirm, formerly so grateful? Not a voice is raised in Your favour! And I, too, whom You have healed, enlightened, resuscitated to grace—I, more guilty than they—I have imitated them; have forgotten Your benefits; have a thousands times preferred vain satisfactions to You.

"He is worthy of death"—*Reus est mortis*. My Jesus, it is I am guilty of death, and it is You they condemn; it is I myself condemn You by the mouth of the Jews. Pilate finds in You no subject of condemnation—*Nullam invenio in Eo causam.* But it is because it is not permitted him to enter into Your Heart; he would there behold the love which has loaded You with our crimes. If the guilty is to escape the divine justice, the Innocent, the God of all sanctity made Man, is worthy of death, because He made Himself a sinner for us, as the Apostle says. O mystery of justice and love! Permit me also to say to You, but with very different sentiments from this guilty people—May Your Blood, this precious Blood, through which we are delivered and saved, fall on us, wash away the stains of our sins; may It inebriate us with grief and love!

Preface.

Jesus hears the sentence of death pronounced; He is loaded with His Cross, He carries it. He listens respectfully to the sentence of God, proclaimed on earth by impious men; He receives it with love. At last He is to be baptized with this baptism of Blood, impatiently longed for by His Heart, burning to repair the outraged glory of His Father and to save guilty man. If one of the Apostles saluted the instrument of his death with these touching expressions—" O good cross, long desired, ardently loved, incessantly sought after, and now prepared for my ardent longings, I come to you full of joy;" what must have been the ardour of Jesus—of this great Heart, which inspires all the generous sentiments of the Saints. Oh, how sweet is this Cross to Him, although He falls three times under His burden! But what fills His Heart with bitterness, what in some manner exhausts His strength, are the sins of the world, which He bears with the Cross; that innumerable multitude of souls who *will* not profit by His sufferings; who will fight against Him, hate Him; and, despite His love, despite His painful death, precipitate themselves into the eternal abyss. Let *us* at least love Him; let *us* carry our cross with Him; let all our moments be consecrated to work, pray, suffer, for the salvation of those dear souls whose interest alone occupied His thoughts, His affections, during His life, amidst His torments, and even to His last sigh upon the Cross.

O Mary, make me a participator in the sentiments by which your Heart was wrung when you met your beloved Son walking to execution, loaded like another Isaac with the wood on which His love was to consume Him. Your Heart could alone comprehend that of Jesus, compassionate the extent of His grief; I offer it to Him to make amends for the inconceivable insensibility of mine.

At the Canon.

Jesus arrives at the summit of Mount Calvary; He is stripped of His clothes and nailed to the Cross.

Jesus is come to the place of sacrifice; His Heart blesses and calls to salvation the entire world, which He considers with a look of tenderness from the summit of the mountain. *Misereor super turbam*—" I have compassion on the multitude;" embracing in thought every nation and individual that compose it in general and particular. He beheld *me* among this innumerable multitude; He distinguished *me*, He blessed *me*.

"If the Just Man shall lay down His life for sin, He shall see a long-lived seed," said the Prophet of our Saviour's Passion—*Si posuerit pro peccato animam suam, videbit semen longævum.** Behold, O Holy Father, the Just by excellence, Who is going to sacrifice His life to You! Oh, give Him in return all those kingdoms, all those souls bought at so great price, give Him the soul of the wretch praying at His feet.

Jesus is brutally stripped of His garments, dumb as a sheep before His shearer, in presence of His executioners, of His creatures, whom one look of His could annihilate. He offers no complaint, no reproach—*Non habens in ore suo redargutiones.* O Jesus, what a lesson—what confusion for me. The least suffering, the slightest sign of haughtiness, the most simple word of command, even on the part of those who hold authority over me, makes my proud and impatient heart so easily rebel.

The Cross is there; Jesus is told to lie down on it. He obeys. They seize His feet, and with inconceivable pain bury enormous nails therein. He presents Himself each of His hands to this intolerable torture. The Blood flows from His painful wounds. Mary, His Mother, assists at this spectacle, heartrending even to the most indifferent.

Oh, could you penetrate into her Heart, hear there the echo of the blows of the hammer which fasten Jesus to the Cross, enter into this sea of bitterness, comprehend the part your own sins added, detest them, deplore them like your Mother! Mary, you will, you can obtain this for your child, who earnestly implores it of you.

* Isaias liii. 10.

At the Elevation.

Jesus is raised on the Cross. The Cross falls with a frightful shock into the hole prepared for it in the rock. Jesus begins the three hours' agony which was to terminate His dolorous Passion. Darkness is over the earth, and compels the Jews to respect the last prayer of an expiring Deity. Jesus utters His seven words, which are as a testament of His mercy and love. Listen to them as if you heard them from His lips at the foot of the Cross, and they were pronounced for you alone.

"Father, forgive them, for they know not what they do."

My Jesus, it is thus You revenge Yourself on Your executioners; You implore their pardon, You excuse them. O my Saviour, pardon poor sinners, of whom I am the first. Ah! too true, we know not what we do when we sin; we know not how grievous it is to outrage a God Who loves us with so generous a love. Make us understand it now, at the foot of Your Cross.

"Woman, behold thy son; son, behold thy Mother."

The silence of Calvary is only broken by the sighs of Mary; they complete the sorrows of of Jesus' Heart, Who wished to suffer alone, and yet this Divine Saviour adds to this ocean of bitterness, as if He had already ceased to exist. He says to Mary—"Behold thy son," showing her the Disciple whom He loved, and to John— "Behold thy Mother." Oh, what agony for Mary's Heart, what painful joy for the Disciple who is going to lose his beloved Master! Holy Virgin, how dearly your love for mankind has cost you! Never can you forget the children of your grief, the last bequest of your expiring Son. Receive into your arms your guilty children.

v

"This day thou shalt be with Me in Paradise."

My Jesus, how easy it is to soften You. The smallest return of heart towards You disarms Your justice. Oh, I implore the same grace as this happy thief, who has the honour to die at Your side—*Peto quod petivit latro pœnitens*. But the Paradise I wish, I desire, is Your Heart; permit me to take up my abode therein, for time and eternity.

"My God, My God, why hast Thou forsaken Me?"

O inconceivable complaint, my Jesus! truly You took upon You even our most afflicting trials! You, the well-beloved Son, abandoned by the most tender of Fathers! What a martyrdom for Your Heart! All is not then lost, when the soul seeking You seems deprived of all support, even in Heaven! You deigned to be abandoned in Your pains, in order that we might not be forsaken in our sins, in order that in the depth of our afflictions we might be able to repeat after You those words rendered all-powerful by Your sacred lips—" My God, My God, why hast Thou forsaken Me?"

"I thirst."—Desire of Holy Communion.

Listen to Jesus, Who says to you from this tabernacle, as formerly from the summit of the Cross—" O soul that I love, I thirst for your salvation, for your perfection, for your love; give Me to drink"—*Da mihi bibere*. Answer Him—" Ah, how can You Who are God ask of me to drink, who am but a poor, weak, miserable, imperfect, sinful creature! 'How dost Thou, being a Jew, ask of me to drink, who am a Samaritan woman?'* How

---

* St. John iv. 9.

can You sigh for so cold a heart as mine? Ah, rather, my Master, I sigh for You, I desire You, the fountain of life. Ah, when shall I go, when appear at Your holy Table, where You slake our thirst with Your Blood? When will You inflame me with this ardent thirst which allowed Your Saints to seek, to desire, to see, to love but You alone? Come, quench my thirst; come, that I may be satiated; come, that my hunger and thirst may be increased!"

Thanksgiving.

"All is consummated. Father, into Thy hands I commend My Spirit."

O Jesus, the God of Calvary, wounded, bruised for my sins, it is You I hold, I possess, in the bottom of my heart! O dull sanctuary, miserable altar; with reason should You prefer Your painful Cross! There, at least, You were surrounded by the three most loving hearts You created—Mary, who surpasses in perfection and love all Heaven itself; John, whom You loved with a love of predilection, and who loved You; Magdalen, to whom You had forgiven many sins by giving her much love. But here, O Jesus, You complain that of all those who assist at this Sacrifice, there is not one who repasses in mind Your agony and sufferings—*Nullus est qui recogitet corde;* and I, alas! though possessing You so intimately, beholding You expire in such torture, *I*, hardly do I think of You, or love You! Would I even be able to count the wanderings of my mind during the Sacrifice You have just offered on this altar? Ah, I hear You say to me—"All is consummated; I have accomplished all the decrees of My Father, all the designs of My love, all the prophecies, to the last tittle.

All My thoughts, all My affections, every moment of My life, has been devoted to you; I shrunk from no ignominy, from no suffering; I gave you even My life in the most intolerable agony; I give Myself daily to you in My Sacrament. Can you say as much? Have you accomplished all the resolutions which gratitude and fervour so frequently inspired you with? Or have you only fulfilled what duty rigorously required of you? Oh, what little effect My example had on you! How great reason I should have to complain, to abandon you, if My love did not prevail over My justice!"

When not Communicating Sacramentally.

"I am smitten as grass, and my heart is withered, because I forgot to eat my bread. Through the voice of my groaning my bone hath cleaved to my flesh" (Psalm ci. 5, 6).

O Jesus, if I passed a day without taking nourishment for my body, what would be my exhaustion; how all my thoughts would turn involuntarily towards the food claimed by necessity! Alas! miserable that I am; I pass days, weeks, months without receiving You. I forget to take the nourishment of my soul, and observe it not, desire it not, make no effort to render myself worthy of it; not a sign escapes me to express regret for the privation. Each day, if I wish, is shown to me, is offered me, the Bread of Heaven, containing within Itself all delights, and I keep aloof, not through respect, but through indifference, tepidity, sloth. It is thus I frustrate all the generous designs of Your love. If You give Yourself daily, is it not because You desire we should receive You daily? And how few reply to this invitation. Happy the souls who hear this voice, who answer it. They approach

You, they enrich themselves with You, while I remain in my misery, hunger, and thirst; my heart dries up; you mingle ashes in the pleasures I desire to take far from You, and tears amidst my joy. To-day, come into my soul; hear my prayer; listen to my cries; turn not away Your face from me; give ear to me, for I know my days vanish like smoke, diminish like a shadow, and if I profit not of the few days you have allotted me upon earth; I shall enter with empty hands into the house of my eternity, where neither wisdom, nor prudence, nor counsel can shelter, from Your justice, any one who has allowed the advances of Your love to remain unanswered.

At the Ablutions.

The sepulchre, the dwelling you wish for time and eternity, is the heart of man, which You created to be Your residence, which You formed after the likeness of Your Divinity, in order that it might be less unworthy of its high destiny. O Jesus, give me Your Heart, then; mine will be worthy of You; inclose me in Your sepulchre; inclose me in Your Heart. There let my life be hidden from the whole world; let no one be acquainted with my glorious sepulture; may I constantly make use of the invisible Food which You reserve for Your friends in this solitude, and may I always be there where I love to remain, rather than where I appear to labour, speak, act, suffer, live, and die.

At the Benediction of the Priest.

Jesus is inclosed in the sepulchre.

O new Moses, bless me with that blessing of the three hours which You gave to the entire world,

Exercise to unite one to the Passion.

when, with arms extended, and held by those nails that fastened You to the Cross, You blessed Your Elect, whom You behold in advance combating for You, disputing, after Your example, with the world, the flesh, and the devil, and, through You, gaining the victory.

May the Sacred Heart of Jesus and the Immaculate Heart of Mary be known, praised, blessed, loved, and glorified for ever! (One hundred days each time.)

the Blessed Virgin Mary

The month of May

Consecrated to the glory of the Mother of God, the Queen of Heaven, etc